Privacy

Defending an Illusion

Martin R. Dowding

THE SCARECROW PRESS, INC.
Lanham • Toronto • Plymouth, UK
2011

Published by Scarecrow Press, Inc.
A wholly owned subsidiary of
The Rowman & Littlefield Publishing Group, Inc.
4501 Forbes Boulevard, Suite 200, Lanham, Maryland 20706
http://www.scarecrowpress.com

Estover Road, Plymouth PL6 7PY, United Kingdom

British Library Cataloguing in Publication Information Available

Library of Congress Cataloging-in-Publication Data

Dowding, Martin Ridley.
Privacy : defending an illusion / Martin R. Dowding.
p. cm.
Includes bibliographical references and index.
ISBN 978-0-8108-8102-0 (pbk. : alk. paper) — ISBN 978-0-8108-8103-7 (ebook)
1. Privacy, Right of. I. Title.
JC596.D69 2011
323.44'8—dc22 2011006016

Contents

Appendixes

Introduction

It has been more than ten years since Sun Microsystems CEO Scott McNealy said, "You have zero privacy anyway . . . get over it."[1] More recently, Facebook founder Mark Zuckerberg wondered whether there is a new, transformed social norm of privacy.[2] McNealy was referring to what he thought our society has done by embracing information and communication technology (ICT), with the effect that we are observed or intruded upon at every electronic corner. Zuckerberg, on the other hand, was asking if people today think privacy is not as *necessary* in the way it was once thought to be necessary. We might also wonder how McNealy and Zuckerberg would respond to "WikiLeaks,"[3] the emerging political crisis that will, undoubtedly, contribute to a new privacy and surveillance norm.

Can those of us who think that privacy is still important maintain our privacy under the contemporary social, legal, and technical conditions just cited? Can we agree on how to maintain privacy? In our current information technology economy, is privacy an illusion? What McNealy and Zuckerberg aren't acknowledging is that many people still believe that there is an ethical, moral, political, and common-sense case for privacy. Information and communication technology *can* expose users to serious harm when their personal information is disclosed. Personal information has value, whether it is disclosed carelessly by users themselves, compromised by others who feel no need to protect someone else's information, or stolen or sold for economic advantage.

Because new technologies are exposing private information in new ways on an almost daily basis, I make no effort in this book to address or resolve every possible privacy violation; however, I do hope to provide some of the information you need to do the following:

- be aware of when and how your privacy is at risk
- know the possible implications of those situations
- learn about some of the legislation and policy that affects the use of information
- evaluate the best means to protect your information, as well as the information of others

Consider the following examples of what happens when personal information falls into the wrong hands in unexpected or unanticipated ways. Losing your wallet may sound simple enough. We hope for the kindness of strangers to resolve such a loss with a phone call. But what if the strangers are not so kind and they decide to make your personal information their own, at least for the duration of its value to them? They could go on a rapid spending spree with a credit card or call around the world if you happen to have a phone card. Or they could do something much worse, for example, using your social security number (or in Canada, your social insurance number) to "become" you by committing identity theft. Using your identity they could take out loans or mortgages for which you would be responsible or commit crimes for which you would be blamed. What if your debit card passwords or credit card numbers are "skimmed" or otherwise "captured" by some device in a store or a gas station? It has happened to me. It has happened to my family and friends.

What if your bodily privacy is compromised when you travel by air or across borders? How do you respond when a complete stranger has the "right" to feel your entire body? What is your response to x-ray scanner technology that exposes more about your body than you want exposed?

What can you do to secure your information on your computer when others have access to it by hacking or spyware? Why, you might wonder, is there porn all over your screen? How can you protect yourself if you have saved romantic e-mails, personal health information, or innocent coursework searches about religion or al-Qaeda that some government agency considers suspicious? What do you do when your parents discover that you have left your Facebook site open and they find out who your "friends" really are and what you really like to do with them? You may have to "talk" about it. What happens to your territorial privacy when your landlord goes into your apartment and rifles through your personal belongings?

Privacy: Defending an Illusion, directed toward senior undergraduates, master's students, and the interested public, has evolved from more than ten years of studying and teaching the history, necessity, and virtues of privacy in a range of societies, businesses, and personal undertakings. Although the book does not entirely agree with what Scott McNealy and Mark Zuckerberg have said about privacy, it does show how changing technology may mean that we *will* have to "get over it." Those who still like their privacy as an "old fashioned" norm will find that they are never alone.

This book is composed of three main parts. The first section is a history of interpretations of privacy in a wide variety of sociocultural circumstances. The second section represents the way ICT has changed our conceptions about privacy and redirected our focus from keeping information private to sharing it with many more people than we would have even a few years ago. The second section also examines a variety of possible options for the future of privacy. The third part of the book, a series of appendixes, encourages debate about privacy.

The book's nine chapters provide a background for defining, understanding, and defending privacy in a wide variety of contexts. Chapter 1 investigates privacy historically, starting with the first known writing about it in classical Greek and Roman texts. These texts created a foundation for later philosophical and political models, including medieval, early modern, enlightenment, modern, and contemporary beliefs. Chapter 2 includes two contrasting narratives about privacy: a pre-ICT view of privacy in the Victorian era and a contemporary day-in-the-life of an everyman in today's wired society.

Chapter 3 introduces the largest sociotechnical challenge to privacy and reviews how Scott McNealy's proclamation about ICT continues to be challenged by social scientists, computer specialists, governments, and legal and cultural analysts committed to privacy. The following chapters address the ways in which different sectors of society are responding to longstanding views about privacy as those views have been transformed by new information and communication technologies. Each section includes approaches taken by the United States and Canada to privacy legislation and policies pertinent to each sector. The internationally recognized Canadian Standards Association's *Model Code for the Protection of Personal Information* and the Organisation for Economic Co-operation and Development's equivalent *Guidelines on the Protection of Privacy and Transborder Flows of Personal Data*, used to design and interpret privacy policies, are included as appendixes to assist readers in designing their own policies and understanding policies they encounter.

Chapter 4 reviews the way governments, claiming to be mindful of privacy, have deployed ICT and observed corporate ICT deployment. Governments also continue to craft privacy policy and legislation to defend users and control corporations' and social networking services' attention to privacy. Chapter 5 issues a warning about how, in spite of its claims to protect privacy, the state uses ICT to circumvent privacy with surveillance techniques and technologies.

Chapters 6 and 7 turn to everyday life after the introduction of ICT. Chapter 6 emphasizes why trust in privacy is vital. The influence of ICT on the private citizen (the body and health) is addressed in chapter 7. Social networking is the subject of chapter 8. And in chapter 9, I speculate on the future of privacy.

The remainder of *Privacy: Defending an Illusion* is composed of a series of appendixes (including material for debate and examples of policies), a section for further reading, and an index. These sections provide resources for readers who want to analyze their own concerns about privacy.

NOTES

1. Polly Sprenger, "Sun on Privacy: 'Get Over It.'" *Wired Magazine*, January 26, 1999. Accessed from www.wired.com/print/politics/law/news/1999/01/17538.
2. Tony Bradley, "Zuckerberg Comments Underscore Conflict between Social Networking and Privacy." *PC World*, January 11, 2010. Accessed from www.pcworld.com/businesscenter/article/186651/zuckerberg.
3. WikiLeaks, http://213.251.145.96/. At the time of this writing, this is the URL for WikiLeaks. This may change daily or have been closed down altogether, given the delicate relationship WikiLeaks has with governments and Web entities.

1

Privacy: From Space to Cyberspace

Privacy has a long and varied history in many cultures. Privacy has been debated by philosophers, poets, anthropologists, political scientists, legal experts, communication scholars, governments, and nongovernmental organizations. Definitions of privacy have changed as moral codes and social opportunities have changed. More recently, new technologies, particularly contemporary information and communication technologies (ICTs), have blurred what is public and what is private, and what can and should be accessible, and in the process have transformed attitudes toward privacy and privacy practices. As a result, there really is no single, simple definition of privacy; however, some significant authors throughout history have defined privacy in political, social, moral, and personal terms.

In his *Politics* (350 BCE), Aristotle distinguishes the public sphere, associated with political activity (*polis*), from the private sphere (*oikis*), associated with the domestic life and the family, and he assigns value (or "virtues") to each sphere. Hannah Arendt, who dedicates a chapter to the "public and private realm" in *The Human Condition*,[1] holds that privacy is no more than a "necessity" and, therefore, not a realm that promotes virtue. She claims that, as Western society developed, a "blurred" concept of privacy evolved that was "social" and not really public or private, as in Aristotle's sense:

> [T]he emergence of the social realm, which is neither private nor public, strictly speaking, is a relatively new phenomenon whose origin coincided with the emergence of the modern age and found its political form in the nation-state.[2]

Judith A. Swanson[3] offers a different view that defends the role of privacy, as Aristotle sees it, when she says,

> For Aristotle, the raison d'etre of privacy is to enable one to turn away . . . to achieve excellence. . . . His account suggests, moreover, that human beings carry virtues earned in private into the public, whereas the human propensity to cherish what is one's own and desirable protects the private from being corrupted by opinions learned in public.[4]

However, Arendt further points out that in the 1950s we understood privacy to be a state of intimacy, rather than a place where we perfected our "virtues." The idea of privacy as intimacy, she said, was introduced to us by Jean-Jacques Rousseau in the eighteenth century, a position shared by Margaret Ogrodnick, who observes that "Rousseau also places higher value on private life as the more faithful indicator of true character."[5] Jürgen Habermas, who cites both Arendt and Rousseau as contributing to our ideas of the private, has devoted much of his career to studying public and private spheres as they have been transformed historically due to a variety of social and political functions and market capitalism.[6]

Also exploring the public/private dichotomy, John Stuart Mill (1992) asks,

> What, then, is the rightful limit to the sovereignty of the individual over himself? Where does the authority of society begin? How much of human life should be assigned to individuality, and how much to society?[7]

Anthropologists report ritualistic seclusion as a sign of a culture's need for privacy during female and male maturation, in periods of mourning, and as preparation for taking on positions of power. The need for withdrawal of young women in Samoan society is well known in the work of anthropologist Margaret Mead. For centuries, young men in many North American Indian tribes were required to seek their "dream vision" before taking on positions of authority. Near Manitoulin Island in northern Ontario, Canada, the famous "Dreamer's Rock" is where

> upon reaching puberty, Indian boys of the surrounding area were sent to the summit where they fasted and, through dreams, received powers from a "guardian spirit." The spirit would also advise them of their calling.[8]

While spirituality and intimacy are still important in our day-to-day lives, we are now in a far different era of interpreting privacy due to advances in information technology (IT). Since World War II, as computers have become more refined, there has been a massive explosion of data collected, distributed, used, and abused in manners unforeseen before the advent of IT. The data explosion was first seen in huge databases of personal information held by governments and corporations. More recently, access to personal ICTs, in the form of PCs, iPhones, and so forth, has culminated in widespread social networking. As a result, Scott McNealy perceives privacy as having disappeared,[9] and Mark Zuckerberg suggests that it has been transformed into a different social norm.[10]

I will describe the multiple kinds of privacy throughout the book by adopting the foundational definitions developed by the London think tank Privacy International, which show that ideas of historic and contemporary privacy can be divided into four main aspects, some of which are more appropriate to particular social and technological conditions, social situations, and historic periods than others. All of the definitions are interrelated but are not necessarily always present or connected. They are as follows:

- *Information privacy:* Involves the establishment of rules governing the collection and handling of such personal data as credit information and medical and government records. It is also known as "data protection."
- *Bodily privacy:* Concerns the protection of people's physical selves against such invasive procedures as genetic testing, drug testing, and body cavity searches.
- *Privacy of communications:* Covers the security and privacy of mail, telephones, e-mail, and other forms of communication.
- *Territorial privacy:* Concerns the setting of limits on intrusion into such domestic and other environments as the workplace or public space. This includes searches, video surveillance, and ID checks.[11]

All of these aspects play a role in the interpretation and protection of privacy today, given that we now live in a so-called information economy that privileges information transfer and technologies to which governments, institutions, and individuals have access. Frequently, one or more (or all) of the kinds of privacy defined come into play simultaneously as social, policy, or legal issues. I will use the Privacy International model, as well as other models introduced in chapter 4, to define a variety of privacy issues throughout the book.

Let's begin with the history of privacy as a general social relationship and then turn to issues that form the background for society's current challenges to privacy, founded on ICT. I will first address territorial and bodily privacy before turning to the effects of cyberspace on privacy.

BODILY AND TERRITORIAL PRIVACY

Aristotle pointed out that there is a public political sphere and a separate private sphere; however, given his privileged position in Athenian society, he was speaking of his own life (and others like his) and not about slaves or other "things" that, in being owned, had no choice but to be public objects. Nor was he speaking of the bleak life of soldiers, particularly in Sparta, where young boys at the age of seven were sent to military and athletic schools where they slept, bathed, and ate together without any of what we would call "territorial" or "bodily privacy." Aristotle's privileged existence allowed him to see life as an individual—or to observe that one could be an individual. That privileged condition continued to be reflected in the literature of Roman poets Horace, Virgil, Martial, and Claudian, all of whom wrote about the positive benefits of "rural retirement."

After the decline of the Roman Empire, during the medieval period, such privileged seclusion went into decline. The Catholic Church began the tradition of "confession," which required that all secrets and transgressions to be divulged to a priest. Living conditions in Europe dictated a life with few secrets and secret behavior, even for aristocrats. Consider the following description of the lack of individual, bodily, and territorial privacy in the medieval period:

> One aspect of Medieval life that is hard for twentieth-century people to comprehend is the lack of individualism and privacy. Both of these characteristics can be accounted for largely by a relative poverty and the fact that most people lived close to the edge of survival. . . . Privacy and individualism are relatively recent developments. In the Medieval period, there was little room, literally, for privacy. The cramped living quarters, even for most nobles, and the lack of central heating, did much to foster togetherness. It was not uncommon for nobles to have huge beds (up to twelve feet wide) that allowed a noble, his wife, their children, some servants, and key members of the lord's "fellowship" (his knights) to sleep together in the dead of Winter.[12]

However, during warmer periods, the traditional structure of a noble's house, with a grand hall dividing the "high" and "low" social ends of the house, meant the development of a sense of separation, if not privacy.

It is also interesting to compare the living arrangements of the indigenous peoples of the Americas. When Columbus and subsequent explorers, priests, and plunderers first encountered Native peoples ("Indians") in the Americas (in what was considered the "uncivilized" world), they were confused by the way the newly "discovered" peoples lived, without contemporary "European" privacy provided by clothing. They discovered housing similar to the medieval hall structure, but with some significant differences. For example, the Iroquoian and Huron people lived in houses without rooms. According to archaeologist Mima Kapches, the "longhouses" looked and functioned in the following manner:

> Based on ethnographic accounts, the longhouse has a nonspecific functional interior. There are no special-function rooms that can be isolated, except for community shared end-storage cubicles. The interior of the house was used by multiple families conducting the same range of domestic and ceremonial activities. Although it is assumed that two families, on opposite sides of the house, shared a hearth, there is no indication of physical partitions delimiting space on Ontario [Canada] sites.[13]

For sixteenth-century Europeans, this type of communal life was no longer typical. By this point, privacy in Europe was becoming an issue of personal individualism, albeit inherent in hierarchy and privilege. That is, there began to be a separation of the public and private spheres, or a "transformation" of those spheres, as Habermas has described it. The most obvious transformation toward privacy in England appeared first in the architectural evolution of upper-class houses in the sixteenth through eighteenth centuries as higher concentrations of wealth allowed for more "seclusion," as described by Nicholas Cooper.[14] In the literature that addresses country houses historically, we find descriptions of the houses themselves that, due to their external opulence, created an image of privacy and exclusivity.[15] Cooper points to class privilege as continuing the trend toward privacy *within* houses of the gentry and aristocracy as changing manners and "civility" called for separate rooms for dressing and specific domestic activities. Despite the privilege of privacy, it should be pointed out that servants invaded their masters' privacy, either by way of being ever present, by helping (or not) to conceal their masters' adulterous affairs, or outright theft.[16]

Wealth allowed a gentleman and his family (and servants) to be isolated and self-sufficient in their country house and gardens. Such lives were celebrated by seventeenth-century English poets who, looking back to classical literature and culture, translated the works of Roman poet-scholars Horace, Virgil, Martial, and Claudian. Many seventeenth-century poets began to write their own contemporary works celebrating the joy of retiring to the country.[17]

In her article "An Englishman's Home Is His Castle? Thresholds, Boundaries, and Privacies in the Eighteenth-Century London House," Amanda Vickery[18] cites the important work of French cultural historian Philippe Ariès, who claims that the social concept of privacy began in England as the introspection of the family, especially due to the concern for children, induced people to move indoors.[19] Vickery also points to the concern feminists and other scholars have about the concealment of the family in the private home with the potential for unseen abuse and conflict. With that Vickery observes that privacy is not always a good thing, especially for those without power. In this sense, she points out that, for the wealthy, "access to privacy was an index of power."[20] And citing the reassessment of the public/private dichotomy of Habermas, who initially spoke little of women's role in the public/private sphere, she makes it clear that the private sphere in eighteenth-century England was spoken about according to particular social groups individually and not necessarily in a comparative way by sex or class.

Patrick H. Hutton[21] observes that, for Ariès, contemporary challenges to privacy stem from the diminishing interactions caused by the decline of the socializing effects of the family, which have been replaced by new technologies and mass society/communication:

> In the affluence of postwar society, [the family] came to covet material possessions in an open-ended way. . . . The effect was to trivialize the socializing role the family had formerly provided for its children. . . . In a poignant way, Ariès noted the private retreat from the obligations of child rearing paralleled the public retreat from involvement in civic affairs. The contemporary family thus jeopardized the mediating role it had previously played between private and public life.[22]

INFORMATION AND COMMUNICATIONS PRIVACY

Forms of control of information and communications began in the earliest societies, but since the rise of information technologies, challenges to privacy have accelerated. In "Timeline: A History of Privacy in America, 1600–2008," Robert Ellis Smith[23] describes Americans' "private" lives in relation to social life and technological advances and points out that in the 1600s the

> clergy, who keep records of births, marriages, and deaths, cast an ever widening net for information about civic affairs. In Massachusetts, "tythingmen," or government watchdogs, inspected households for proper moral conduct. . . . Under Puritan rules it was a civic duty to keep an eye on your neighbor. In many towns, people were forbidden from living alone.[24]

In the 1700s "mail was routinely opened as it passed through the postal system."[25] But by this time, as America began to define itself as it overcame its colonial status, "private life was seen as a haven from public turmoil . . . a man's house is his castle."[26] In 1791, the "Bill of Rights protected freedom of speech and freedom from unreasonable search and seizure"; however, in 1838, the first electronic form of communication, the telegraph, was introduced, and the "bugging of telegraphed messages began."[27] Around 1900, "fingerprints were established as unique and unchangeable identifiers."[28]

At this juncture, the significant influence of information technologies on privacy (and privacy policy) began to appear. Smith cites a foundational article by U.S. Supreme Court justices Samuel D. Warren and Louis D. Brandeis entitled "The Right to Privacy,"[29] published in 1890. The article is an argument against the invasive use of cameras in public and is written in favor of the "right to be let alone." Smith's entry for 1928 points to the U.S. Supreme Court's ruling that the "seizure of electronic conversations [including by telephone] is constitutional."[30] In 1968, the Omnibus Crime Control and Safe Streets Act, Title III (sometimes referred to as the "end of privacy"), "specifies when a warrant is required for wiretapping." Between 1978 and 1994, Congress passed refinements to the wiretapping laws that required telecommunications companies to be "wiretap-ready." Smith also cites an earlier article, "Cryptography and Computer Privacy,"[31] which ominously portends that "there is growing concern that computers now constitute, or will soon constitute, a dangerous threat to individual privacy."[32] In 2001, the USA Patriot Act granted authorities "broad discretion to search databases and conduct surveillance."[33] And the final entry, for 2008, acknowledges that "Congress updated the 1978 wiretapping law, expanding the surveillance powers of the executive branch."[34] In the midst of intrusive and constantly changing technologies and changing attitudes, is privacy an *illusion* about which we should be concerned?

Based on the increasing concentration concerning "privacies" in a wide variety of academic disciplines, including anthropology, communication studies, computer science, health studies, law, social work, and psychology, privacy has clearly become one of the most challenging ethical conundrums in contemporary science and social science research. And, given the daily media reports, personal blog entries, and association websites dedicated to threats to privacy, it is clear that it is not only something that the "Ivory Tower" is concerned about. It appears that we all are—or at least should be—concerned, as I demonstrate throughout the rest of this book. But why now, and what has caused the change?

If we can "blame" anything, I venture that it is the fault of how contemporary ICT so persuasively demonstrates Harold Innis's theory of "space bias." As Innis's theory makes clear, the faster and farther a message can travel, from a running man carrying papyrus, to fiber optic cable carrying information at the speed of light, the faster ideology, rumor, gossip, and misinformation can travel. We may also now live in Marshall McLuhan's "global village," but like any village (as opposed to a large, cosmopolitan city), we are coming to know too much about too many people, too often, via rumor, gossip, misinformation, and, moreover, misinterpretation of information, through the effects of ICT.

Whereas there were once discrete pre-ICT literatures that addressed privacy in terms of emotional, spiritual, psychological, legal, and moral values, the effects of universally deployed ICT has added a new, overarching way of addressing the issue. As a consequence of the wide-ranging adoption of ICT as a presumed panacea for the safe, fast, and cost-effective exchange of information, virtually every facet of everyday personal and political life can now be gathered, organized, interpreted, and disseminated electronically, as Julian Assange of WikiLeaks and his supporters have made clear.[35]

Consequently, a new literature has emerged, including this book, which concentrates, not on various privacies, but on one "virtual" privacy in light of the influence of ICTs. To further illustrate that transformation, chapter 2 compares and contrasts two narratives, one historical and one contemporary, that show how we have gone from a society most cognitive of territorial privacy to one obsessed with privacy as territorial, bodily, informational, and communicative.

QUESTIONS FOR DISCUSSION

This chapter introduces four privacy domains defined by Privacy International. Consider the following questions based on Privacy International's definitions.

1. Have you had your information privacy breached? What were the implications?
2. Has your bodily privacy been jeopardized by "invasive procedures"?
3. Have the security and privacy of your communications been breached?
4. Has your territorial privacy been intruded upon?
5. Which of the privacy domains named above is most important to you?

NOTES

1. Hannah Arendt, *The Human Condition* (Chicago: University of Chicago Press, 1958).

2. Arendt, *The Human Condition*, 28.

3. Judith A. Swanson, *The Public and the Private in Aristotle's Political Philosophy* (Ithaca, NY: Cornell University Press, 1992).

4. Swanson, *The Public and the Private in Aristotle's Political Philosophy*, 3.

5. See Jean-Jacques Rousseau, *On the Social Contract: Discourse on the Origin of Inequality, Discourse on Political Economy* (Indianapolis, IN: Hackett Publishing, 1983).

6. Jürgen Habermas, *The Structural Transformation of the Public Sphere: An Inquiry into a Category of Bourgeois Society* (Cambridge, MA: MIT Press, 1991).

7. John Stuart Mill, *On Liberty*, chapter IV, "Of the Limits to the Authority of Society over the Individual" (New York: Knopf, 1992), 72. Originally published in 1859.

8. Dreamer's Rock is recognized with a plaque on Birch Island. The quotation is taken from the plaque, placed at the location in 1971 by the Ontario Heritage Trust, an agency of the government of Ontario.

9. Polly Sprenger, "Sun on Privacy: 'Get Over It.'" *Wired Magazine*, January 26, 1999. Accessed from www.wired.com/print/politics/law/news/1999/01/17538.

10. Facebook creator Mark Zuckerberg was recently thought to have said that "privacy [is] no longer a 'social norm' and has just evolved over time." "Facebook's Zuckerberg Says the Age of Privacy Is Over." *Telegraph*, January 29, 2009. Accessed from www.telegraph.co.uk/technology/facebook/6966628/Facebooks-Mark-Zuckerberg.

11. Privacy International, "Overview of Privacy." Accessed from www.privacyinternational.org/article.shtml?cmd%5B347%5D=x-347-559474.

12. James F. Dunnigan and Albert A. Nofi, "Medieval Life and the Hundred Years War: Medieval Society and Culture." Accessed from www.hyw.com/Books/History/1/_Help_C.htm.

13. Mima Kapches, "The Spatial Dynamics of Ontario Iroquoian Longhouses." *American Antiquity* 55(1) (1990): 49–67.

14. Nicholas Cooper, "Rank, Manners, and Display: The Gentlemanly House, 1500–1750." *Transactions of the Royal Historical Society* 12(2002): 291–310.

15. Cooper, "Rank, Manners, and Display," 296.

16. See Philippe Ariès and Georges Duby, eds., *A History of Private Life*, Vol. 1 (Cambridge, MA: Belknap Press, 1987), 72–73. See also Lawrence Stone, *Broken Lives: Separation and Divorce in England, 1660–1857* (Oxford, UK: Oxford University Press, 1993), 26–27.

17. A. D. Harvey, "The Roman Ideal of Rural Retirement in Seventeenth- and Eighteenth-Century England." *Contemporary Review* (Autumn 2006): 357–66.

18. Amanda Vickery, "An Englishman's Home Is His Castle?: Thresholds, Boundaries, and Privacies in the Eighteenth-Century London House." *Past and Present* 199(1) (2008): 147–73.

19. Vickery, "An Englishman's Home Is His Castle?," 148.

20. Vickery, "An Englishman's Home Is His Castle?," 167.

21. Patrick H. Hutton, "Late-Life Historical Reflections of Philippe Ariès on the Family in Contemporary Culture." *Journal of Family History* 26(3) (July 2001): 395–410.

22. Hutton, "Late-Life Historical Reflections of Philippe Ariès on the Family in Contemporary Culture," 398–99.

23. Robert Ellis Smith, "Timeline: A History of Privacy in America, 1600–2008." *Scientific American* 299(3) (2008): 50–57.

24. Smith, "Timeline: A History of Privacy in America, 1600–2008," 52–53.

25. Smith, "Timeline: A History of Privacy in America, 1600–2008," 53.

26. Smith, "Timeline: A History of Privacy in America, 1600–2008," 53.

27. Smith, "Timeline: A History of Privacy in America, 1600–2008," 53.

28. Smith, "Timeline: A History of Privacy in America, 1600–2008," 53.

29. Samuel D. Warren and Louis D. Brandeis, "The Right to Privacy." *Harvard Law Review* 4(5) (1890): 193–207. Cited in Smith, "Timeline: A History of Privacy in America, 1600–2008," 53. In this article, Warren and Brandeis articulate one of the first legal arguments against the careless and malicious use of information technology—cameras.

30. Smith, "Timeline: A History of Privacy in America, 1600–2008," 53.

31. Horst Feistel, "Cryptography and Computer Privacy." *Scientific American* 228(5) (1973): 15–23. Cited in Smith, "Timeline: A History of Privacy in America, 1600–2008," 53.

32. Feistel, "Cryptography and Computer Privacy." Cited in Smith, "Timeline: A History of Privacy in America, 1600–2008," 53.

33. Smith, "Timeline: A History of Privacy in America, 1600–2008," 53.

34. Smith, "Timeline: A History of Privacy in America, 1600–2008," 53.

35. WikiLeaks, http://213.251.145.96/.

2

A Contrast between Pre-ICT Privacy and Today's ICT Realities

This chapter introduces two very different fictional scenarios to demonstrate how the concepts of personal space and degrees of trust have been altered by the effects of cyberspace on informational, bodily, communications, and territorial privacy. The first narrative, which Amanda Vickery created from her research on the proceedings of London's Old Bailey criminal court, depicts typical late nineteenth-century working class personal territorial privacy. While London was and remains one of the world's largest cosmopolitan cities, Vickery describes a place and time in which the poor were limited to small neighborhoods and confined living quarters that they often shared with people they barely knew. They had few possessions and were compelled to protect them in ingenious ways. The second narrative, by Wolfgang Sofsky, represents a "day-in-the-life" of a contemporary office worker as he and his son make their way to and from school and work, while, thanks to information and communication technology, their information, bodily, communications, and territorial privacy are recorded and compromised every minute of the day.

TERRITORIAL PRIVACY AND TRUST

From Amanda Vickery, "An Englishman's Home Is His Castle? Thresholds, Boundaries, and Privacies in the Eighteenth-Century London House." Past and Present *199(1) (2008): 148–49. Reprinted with permission.*

The dusk spreads from the river. Candles are lit all over London. The clattering of shuttering echoes and answers as every house in the Georgian metropolis fortifies itself against the advancing dark. The November gloom calls the lodgers home, scurrying back with sausages, oysters, and a pennyworth of tea. At the corner of Shoe Lane in the city, the landlord, a carpenter, is still away at his workshop, and the landlady is seeing her tenants in, unlocking the street door and the individual rooms for her three newest inmates: a laundress, a fruit-seller, and a journeyman cabinetmaker. They exchange words on the cold stairs; she has changed their linen today. (Has she snooped through their things again? Almost certainly.)

In the second-floor front chamber, the journeyman lights his fire and then scuttles next door to fetch his dinner on a tray from the alehouse. Loosening his breeches, he empties his pockets and stashes the coin in the hiding place he has engineered in the leg of the oak bed. Unusually, the landlady's linen press stands open in the corner. She must have forgotten to relock it. The journeyman runs his hands over the second-best sheets, all initialed and numbered with red embroidery silk. Attractive, but he wants a quiet life, and he has had worse quarters than these.

The fruit-seller heats her sausages over the hearth in the second-floor back chamber. Warmer, she idly unlocks her box (she carries the key always in her pocket), checking over her shifts, Sunday best gown, and handkerchiefs. Her small stock of valuables—cash, a watch, a silver teaspoon, and a ring—she keeps always on her person. In the draughty front garret, the young laundress eats her oysters, locks away some ribbons in her box, and hides coins in a hole in the wainscot. Sometimes she has to share her bed with passing girls, and she is no fool.

Presently, the maid of all work leaves to visit a relative by arrangement, and, as the landlady must pop out to the alehouse for beer, she leaves the street door key in the custody of her trusty, a mature needlewoman and widow who rents the first-floor back chamber. The widow can't complain; she holds her own room key and just now is making her supper in the family kitchen, as she has done at this hour every night for the past seven years. Errand accomplished, the landlady takes back her keys, relocks the kitchen, and retreats to the ground-floor parlor to await her husband.

By nine everyone is gathered back in. The apprentice beds down in the back garret with the two little boys of the house, the maid in the warm back kitchen on a truckle bed, her bulging tie-on pockets stuffed under her pillow. At ten, the landlady locks the tenants, servants, and children in their rooms for the night. The landlord hefts the iron bar across the street door, padlocks the door to the back lane, and double-checks the window shutters. Only streetwalkers and housebreakers are lurking about now, he tells his wife, as he lights her to the first-floor front chamber. In their curtained conjugal bed, in shift and shirt, husband and wife rehearse the details of their day. The landlady puts the keys under her pillow and settles to sleep, just as the watch calls out the hour of eleven.

Immediately after the preceding passage Vickery responds to her fictional account by asking, "Where in this story does personal privacy reside?" It resides in the emotional and physical security created by houses and the individual rooms for withdrawal and solitude within them, she says. Challenges to territorial and bodily privacy reside everywhere, as Vickery's language of locking up suggests. Children are locked into their rooms. Personal property is hidden in secret places, either on the person or in "territory" that the inhabitants of Vickery's story feel secure about. Trust is at a premium. People retire to their curtained beds. This is a study in space, privacy, and surveillance.

What follows is a study in cyberspace that brings into play Privacy International's privacy of communications, territorial privacy, information privacy, bodily privacy, and surveillance, indicating how privacy has changed since the full deployment of information and communication technologies.

CYBERSPACE: NO PLACE FOR PRIVACY?

From Wolfgang Sofsky, Privacy: A Manifesto. *Trans. S. Rendall. (Princeton, NJ: Princeton University Press, 2008), 1–7. Reprinted with permission.*

By the time Anton B. left the building in the morning, he'd already been recorded three times. His conversation with his parents had been saved on a telephone company computer. He entered the field of a surveillance camera in the hall the moment he stepped out the door of his apartment. As he was hurrying to the elevator with his four-year-old son, on the ground floor the doorman was going toward the revolving door. Holding one hand behind his back and fumbling with the top button of his blue uniform coat with the other, he smiled at

B. and gave him a nod. Before he made his next round, he straightened his tie and quickly wrote in his record book the time at which B. had left the building.

As B. drove toward the kindergarten, he noticed that the needle on the gas gauge was getting close to the red area. It looked as though new devices had been hung over several intersections during the night. Only at the gas station did B. still see the old video cameras. Now and then the cashier looked over at a little screen that never showed anything but cars, gas pumps, bored passengers, and customers moving around. As usual, B. paid for his gas with his credit card. On the receipt were listed not only the gas but also the newspaper and a bag of licorice that B. handed to his boy, who was begging for the candy. When they got to the kindergarten a few blocks farther on, his son immediately ran happily into the big playroom where a clown's head was mounted on a swivel on the ceiling, its glass left eye peeping down at the room. If B. wanted to see what his son was doing he needed only to boot up the computer in his office.

B. turned on the car radio and put on his sunglasses. Because he was in a hurry, he floored the gas pedal and quickly turned onto the expressway. He had been driving this route for years and knew exactly where the radars were. So he was all the more surprised when he saw a flash as he drove up the on-ramp. Cursing, B. pounded on the steering wheel. Then he remembered that on the toll bridge all license numbers were filmed and compared with those of stolen cars. He didn't notice the infrared flash on the pedestrian bridge. Even before he'd reached his company's underground garage, almost every instant of his existence in the public sphere had been recorded. He entered his office using a card with a computer chip that recorded his arrival time.

B. sat down at his desk and turned on his computer to look at his e-mails. Between the computer and the keyboard there was a little device that recorded all his keystrokes. Although B. was in a position of trust, a key-logger was installed on his machine as well. Employees were allowed to use the Internet, even for their own purposes, but they had to remember that everything they keyed in would be recorded. Most of them, therefore, voluntarily avoided using the company's computers for their private correspondence. The inconspicuous device on the keyboard reminded everyone that, so far as possible, he should keep his secrets to himself.

During the lunch hour, B. got two calls. His tax adviser reported that tax officials had requested a statement regarding a foreign payment. B. was not aware of any irregularity. Apart from a few parking and speeding tickets, he'd never had any problem with the authorities.

However, a year earlier he'd used his credit card to pay a bill at the hotel where he'd spent his vacation. The inquiry suggested that the tax man knew everything that happened in his bank account. Obviously, some official had looked into his affairs without notifying him about it. B. felt a vague concern welling up inside him. He opened the window and looked down on the narrow street below. Music was being played softly over a loudspeaker. Now and then he could hear a strange buzz. It came from a tiny, almost invisible surveillance drone listening for suspicious noises in alleys and side streets.

The second telephone call was from his family doctor, who asked which data B. wanted to be recorded on the new health card. In order to make emergency care easier and decrease costs, the health insurance companies had recently begun to issue each patient a card with a computer chip, on which, along with identification information, all previous diagnoses, treatments, and prescriptions were registered, along with an organ donor agreement. The doctor advised B. to put only the required minimum of information on the card, a proposal that B. immediately accepted, even though he believed the trend toward complete digital records was ultimately unstoppable.

About 1:00 p.m., B. inquired about a train connection for his wife, who was visiting her parents. On the phone, his father-in-law promised him that he would not fail to get his daughter to the train station on time. B.'s company had expressly allowed private calls to be made on B.'s business phone. However, all area codes and numbers were recorded for the monthly telephone bill. In any case, the walls of the offices were so thin that they discouraged conversations that were too confidential or long-winded. B. had long since learned not to mention names when he was on the telephone. But it didn't take a genius to guess the names from the characteristic but inevitable expressions used in a conversation. Around 4:30 p.m., he turned off his computer, put his things in his briefcase, stuck the card with the computer chip in the reader, and descended into the underground garage.

Video cameras in the corridor and in the elevator allowed the company's security guards to know who was currently in the building. On the expressway, B. passed the toll bridge and the pedestrian bridge again before he parked his car in the supermarket lot. Right behind the entrance stood an inconspicuous device the size of a refrigerator, a backscatter x-ray machine that scanned every customer. The screen showed not only what one might be hiding under one's clothes or underwear; one's naked shape also was clearly recognizable. Although B. regularly bought food for the family on his way home and knew every corner of the store, on this particular day he walked helplessly up and down the aisles. At the cash register he hesitated to pull out his credit card. Credit cost him dearly. Every time he bought something, his preferences, whether he tried a new product, and how much money he probably could spend were all recorded.

At the train station, guards in dark blue uniforms checked all suitcases, backpacks, and handbags, sometimes cursorily, sometimes meticulously. The video cameras on the platforms were state-of-the-art. They had microphones and identification filters that triggered an alarm when they detected unusual movements or certain faces. After the recent incidents, railroad officials had hastily installed new devices. According to the official announcement, even the most experienced observer would have been unable to monitor thousands of passengers at the same time. Automatic comparison of the pictures with a photo and video databank, however, took only a millisecond. Using eyebrows, the distance between the eyes, the tip of the nose, and countless other physical characteristics, a suspicious face could immediately be spotted from any point of view. Neither glasses nor beards nor wigs could prevent identification. B. had read about all that in the newspaper. Nonetheless, he wondered about a couple of uniformed guards who were no longer wandering around the waiting room, as they had done earlier, but were now standing conspicuously along the wall. Out of the corner of his eye he saw that at the end of the platform four guards had surrounded a young man. They were pushing him against a guardrail and searching him. Passersby paid little attention; a few looked the other way, and others pretended that they didn't see anything. One shouldn't get involved, people said, everything is all right. Minor arrests are arranged by the authorities.

On the way home, B. and his wife picked up their son at the kindergarten. When the family entered the apartment building, the staff had begun a new shift. The new doorman gave them a friendly smile and wrote down their arrival time. He glanced briefly at the monitor screen and then went back to his crossword puzzle. B. hesitated for a moment. He found it almost impossible to go into the elevator; all of a sudden, it was as if he'd heard a voice that told him to wait. Only when he had closed the door to his apartment did he feel that he was no longer being observed.

After dinner, he booted up his laptop and got on the Internet. Immediately he found himself again the object of attention. His Internet service provider recorded his activities. The websites he visited recorded his data. He had given his e-mail address to a newsgroup, and the auction site where he usually tried to complete his collection of antique toys had registered every one of his transactions over the past month and made them available to everyone who might be interested in them. Every ten minutes a window came up on his screen warning him that his virus definitions were out of date and needed to be updated immediately. Unknown Trojan horses might be collecting information on his computer. B. ordered two books from a bookstore that already had his credit card information. He checked the prices for digital cameras at three sites. His electronic mailbox contained several advertisements sent by companies he'd never heard of.

Before he went to bed, Anton B. spent a moment thinking over the events of the day. A brief malaise came over him as he began to realize that he had not been alone for even a minute.

QUESTIONS FOR DISCUSSION

The following questions challenge issues from chapter 1 that are represented in chapter 2.

1. Can there be a difference between the public and the private, as Aristotle saw the dichotomy so clearly according to Judith A. Swanson[1] in chapter 1?
2. What is life when we can never be alone?
3. Why is Anton B. always under surveillance?
4. Does the "new" privacy, such as it is, represent a "blurred" public and private, not delimited to one side or the other, as Hannah Arendt[2] interpreted Aristotle?

NOTES

1. Judith A. Swanson, *The Public and the Private in Aristotle's Political Philosophy* (Ithaca, NY: Cornell University Press, 1992).
2. Hannah Arendt, *The Human Condition* (Chicago: University of Chicago Press, 1958).

3

Did ICT Create a New Social Norm?

As pointed out in chapter 1 and as is clear from the excerpts in chapter 2, many observers have defined privacy by recognizing a difference between the "public" and the "private" spheres and have noted that, in some contexts, security can be provided by privacy. These observers point out that privacy is often a function of privilege, requires that care be taken to guard it, and derives from a need to withdraw from public society to protect oneself and one's belongings (as Vickery points out in her nineteenth-century narrative). In Sofsky's account of all-encompassing surveillance as envisioned in George Orwell's novel *1984*, the character "Anton B." realizes he has had no such opportunity to withdraw.

Authors cited in chapter 1, particularly Aristotle and his sympathizer Judith A. Swanson,[1] observed that withdrawal to singular solitude—confining oneself to a house or life within a family—once defined the line between the public and private spheres and the virtues derived from that dichotomy. Swanson is particularly adamant about "assimilating Aristotle's teaching about the public and the private, in particular about the centrality of excellence to private activity."[2]

Hannah Arendt's[3] insistence that the "public sphere," a modern concept she says was unthinkable for the ancients,[4] problematizes the Aristotelian dichotomy but introduces a very significant third way of evaluating privacy. Arendt claims that our modern interpretation of privacy derives from a *social* sphere, one that we can investigate in the light of, for example, our modern personal relationships based on individualism and information technologies (IT).

Prior to the advent of information and communication technology (ICT), being "let alone,"[5] as U.S. Supreme Court justices Samuel D. Warren and Louis D. Brandeis put it, was often as simple as not being subject to Anton B.'s life of surveillance. Since the advent and development of electronic information transfer throughout the nineteenth and twentieth centuries and the deployment of current ICT, particularly social networking sites (SNSs), the line between public and private has become blurred and uncertain.

That lack of clarity recently caused many journalists and ICT users to wonder what Facebook CEO and cofounder Mark Zuckerberg meant when he said,

> People have really gotten comfortable not only sharing more information and different kinds, but more openly and with more people. That social norm [privacy] is just something that has evolved over time. We view it as our role in the system to constantly be innovating and be updating what our system is to reflect what the current social norms are.[6]

Some privacy analysts took that to mean that Zuckerberg implied that privacy is dead, while others wondered what "current social norms" are.

Regardless of how "comfortable" some people may now feel about sharing their personal information, many others still simply want to "be let alone." The way personal information is now collected, organized, and transferred via computers, cell phones, and the Internet has meant a vast change in what is private and what is potentially public, as the malaise felt by the character Anton B. portrays. Given how rapidly the norms and expectations of privacy are perceived to be changing, it is not surprising that Mark Zuckerberg's statement caused controversy.

The transformational influence of new media technologies on the collection of information is, however, not new. Issues related to privacy and ICT were first tentatively codified, legally, more than a century ago in the foundational essay by Warren and Brandeis. Their article "The Right to Privacy," published in *The Harvard Law Review*, points out that

> the individual shall have full protection in person and in property is a principle as old as the common law; but it has often been found necessary from time to time to define anew the exact nature and extent of such protection. . . . [R]ecent inventions and business methods call

> attention to the next step [that] must be taken for the protection of the person . . . the right "to be let alone."[7]

Significantly, the "recent inventions and business methods" Warren and Brandeis condemn are "instantaneous photographs and newspaper enterprise," or what was then known as the "yellow" press and today is represented by *The National Inquirer*, *News of the World*, or such websites as Perez Hilton's.[8] Warren and Brandeis's argument is that nineteenth-century "new media" (cheap Kodak cameras) used by mischievous or reckless people can cause harm to reputations. In a contemporary response to the misuse of ICTs, Daniel J. Solove[9] cites the harm done to a person's reputation when privacy is compromised by cell phone camera users, online social networking "friends," or anyone who uses new media indiscriminately.

NEW TECHNOLOGIES: WE ARE ALL VULNERABLE

College students and younger people appear to be most vulnerable to the loss of privacy when using new technologies, partly because they use them more frequently than others, and also because they have used them for most of their lives. Sending photos on cell phones or becoming "friends" with total strangers on SNSs, most notably Facebook (see chapter 8), have become extremely problematic due to the often thoughtless, poorly planned (or simply unanticipated) effects of "sharing" personal information.

The online habits of young people have been closely observed by two cyberspace scholars, John Palfrey, in *Born Digital: Understanding the First Generation of Digital Natives*,[10] and Patricia Sanchez Abril, in "A (My) Space of One's Own: On Privacy and Online Social Networks."[11] Palfrey's work on SNSs introduced the provocative and useful concept of young "digital natives," high school or undergraduate students or recent hi-tech graduates,[12] for example, who were born into the newest media, and "digital immigrants," like "baby boomers" and their parents, who have adapted to new IT. Sanchez Abril challenges Palfrey by saying that many students are not, in fact, tech savvy; their interests are narrowly focused, while many older adults are well versed in ICTs and are more sophisticated in their social networking methods.[13] Both scholars, however, address SNSs as being crucial to privacy research, on one hand providing new forms of communities, but on the other hand, providing new opportunities for reckless behavior.

SOCIAL NETWORKING

Whether one is a new media "native" or "immigrant," there is a lot to learn about privacy and SNSs, especially because privacy policies and settings change frequently and are often impossible to understand due to their length or complex language. Although the nominally savvy "natives," like college undergraduates, may arrive on campus with deeper online experience than their professors, it is often narrower experience with games and SNSs, activities that expose them more often to surveillance and scams than to genuine information.

The older "immigrants" are more than likely to have a better sense of the cost-benefit "individuality" as conceived of by John Stuart Mill in his *On Liberty and Utilitarianism* as a way for people to maximize their social benefits and minimize the social costs.[14] The "natives" also bring to school less awareness of what C. Arthur Van Lear Jr.[15] calls "self-disclosure reciprocity," also related to the cost-benefit of degrees of social engagement. The "immigrants" have, at least, experienced broader social behavior in general and are, therefore, more wary of online dangers and the value of self-preservation. In their relatively brief engagement with privacy problems in day-to-day life, the "natives" are subject to greater attempts at compromising their online privacy than any other generation before them.

In a discussion at the 29th International Conference of Data Protection and Privacy Commissioners in 2007, entitled "The Next Generation Dragon: Children's Online Privacy," presenter Valerie Steeves addressed the effects of such wildly popular children's online cyberworlds as Barbie.com (launched in 2001), Webkinz (launched in 2005), and Neo Pets (launched in 1999).[16] To enter the sites, children are required to reveal a great deal of personal information about their families, including what they eat, what they wear, and other information that will help a corporation behind the game create market profiles. Those sites are potentially harmful, according to Steeves, because they lull children into becoming passive commodities by subjecting them to the interactive marketing of games, products, branding, and corporate behavior.

Because Neo Pets was launched in 1999, millions of undergraduate students entering college have now had more than ten years to become accustomed to giving up their personal information without question. Students who "graduate" to such SNSs as MySpace (launched in 2003) and Facebook (launched in 2004) may bring with them the naïve commitment that they developed through their earlier online experiences and disclose more private information than they realize will be harmful in the future.

SURVEILLANCE, SECURITY, AND REPUTATION

Given Steeves's argument that Internet "natives" may not be aware of dangerous online activity, it is easy to understand why many younger users are not concerned about being recorded by, for example, closed-circuit TV (CCTV). They have already uploaded their photos and shared their unguarded behavior on SNSs. In what could be seen as an effort to control student behavior—or guarantee security—many colleges and universities have increased CCTV coverage to virtually blanket campuses. "Swipe card" entrances have been implemented in many residence halls, study rooms, and classrooms. Eye scan, body scan, or fingerprint impression identification is already being implemented throughout such public spaces as airports and elsewhere. Will such challenges to privacy change behavior? That remains to be seen, but it is somewhat doubtful, given many of the replies I have received during discussions and focus groups I held for this book with citizens, faculty, and students.

Interviewees for this part of the book (mostly students) typically respond to questions about how they feel about surveillance technologies by saying that if they are not engaging in criminal activity, they have nothing to fear. But that answer is only viable in a completely static culture. If behavior does not get worse and surveillance remains the same, the interviewees' replies are correct. And if our relatively liberal political regime(s) continue unchanged, there really is nothing to worry about. But if social, political, or moral norms were to change in the future, or as they already have, according to Mark Zuckerberg, actions that are not considered inappropriate now might be disapproved of by those people who hold to the new norms. So far, despite new media, behavior hasn't changed much, given SNS users' willingness to appear in compromising situations at parties that later appear as film on YouTube or photos on Facebook, situations that are potentially online forever—and are often searched by human resource departments when people apply for jobs.[17]

PRIVACY AND SECURITY

When the CEO of Sun Microsystems, Scott McNealy, said, "You have zero privacy anyway. Get over it," he was referring to the fact that

ICT is vulnerable to hacking and is technically unable to guarantee privacy or confidentiality. While hacking and/or carelessness compromise privacy, so too does the ever-growing reliance on surveillance for what is defined as "security." (Chapter 5 addresses this more fully.) Such laws as Section 215 of the USA Patriot Act, the European Union cybercrime law, or the still-to-be-determined Canadian "lawful access" equivalent drastically challenge our "right to be let alone." At the time of this writing, the Conservative[18] Canadian Government's "lawful access" legislation has been reintroduced after having "died" when Prime Minister Stephen Harper "prorogued" Parliament in 2009. The Conservatives proposed new legislation following efforts by the previous Liberal government to create a surveillance society in light of pressure to fall in line with other international legislation and practice, particularly the United States.[19]

Since the events of September 11, 2001, many of the U.S. security laws that already existed were overwhelmed by the USA Patriot Act, of which Section 215 allows the Federal Bureau of Investigation (FBI) to secretly request and obtain personal information, including business, library, and university records, in any form of media for virtually anyone for any reason or no reason at all. If the FBI merely believes persons are involved in what they suspect to be illegal activity, they can access almost any records. Section 505 of the Patriot Act permits the FBI to obtain records by using National Security Letters (NSL), that is, without warrants; and Section 215 automatically requires, while Section 505 permits, the FBI to impose a "gag" order on persons under investigation. That is, those sections prohibit the reporting of abuse of government authority, which affects one of America's most cherished freedoms—the First Amendment.

Canadians are also affected by the Patriot Act and other related surveillance legislation that grants or denies access to the United States, for example, "no-fly" lists.[20] Section 215 of the Patriot Act determines that the U.S. security apparatus has access to information that has crossed the border (or is "outsourced") to U.S. information storage companies. Canadian companies must agree to follow various pieces of legislation, for example, the North American Free Trade Agreement, or those imposed by the World Trade Organization or other business-related agreements, like the World Intellectual Property Organization, for such purposes as banking, trade, and international criminal law.

Canada's Investigative Powers for the 21st Century Act (IP21C) could, like the Patriot Act, require that Internet service providers (ISPs), including university and college IT services, libraries, and other public institutions, surrender to police all subscribers' personal information without clear justification and without anyone necessarily knowing that he or she is under suspicion or why. IP21C and the Patriot Act would also require ISPs to preserve data that users have saved on their systems (though it is not certain for how long), increasing the amount of computer space needed to store the data and imposing an added cost and responsibility to keep that information secure for government access.

But, in the post-9/11 era, how much privacy is the Canadian Government (or any government, for that matter) willing to take away to attempt to guarantee security? There is a difficult balance to achieve. Canada is a globalized and increasingly militarized country situated next to the United States.[21] The U.S. security apparatus impinges on Canada (and other countries) daily, either at the border, within the United States, or even in Canada if our information is held in U.S. databases. The effect of the U.S. surveillance apparatus is proving that great vigilance is required to maintain such cultural "traditional" norms as privacy (providing that Canada's own "lawful access" legislation doesn't contradict or diminish its own privacy regime). Such vigilance, or at least a foundation for it, is provided by international agreements, including Article 12 of the 1948 United Nations Declaration of Human Rights and such national laws as the Fourth Amendment of the U.S. Constitution and Sections 7 and 8 of Canada's Charter of Rights and Freedoms, all of which acknowledge the right to privacy. And privacy "watchdogs" (or more correctly in Canada, "commissioners") work at arm's length from government to advise citizens about privacy law and policy and respond to freedom of information requests and breaches of privacy. Chapter 4 addresses these issues further.

WHY WE NEED PRIVACY WATCHDOGS

There are many reasons why such privacy watchdogs as state, provincial, and national privacy commissioners, university ombudspersons, and privacy officers in institutions are important. This section provides one example, and others will be introduced in sections related to specific issues, including in the workplace and surveillance. An important concern is freedom of research, in particular the storing of Canadian electronic academic records on U.S. computer servers. Many Canadian academic institutions subscribe to RefWorks, an electronic research service. According to its webpage, "RefWorks, an online research management, writing, and collaboration tool, is designed to help researchers easily gather, manage, store, and share all types of information, as well as generate citations and bibliographies."[22]

The U.S. servers, and the Canadian researchers' data stored on them, were subject to the unknown and unknowable effects of Section 215 of the Patriot Act.[23] That section, which allowed "unwarranted" searches of data, breached Canadian universities' trust in their relationship with the U.S. security apparatus. Given the secrecy of Section 215 of the Patriot Act, we will never know if the FBI looked, what they were looking for, or what they found.

While RefWorks' promise to "easily gather, manage, store, and share all types of information" sounded attractive, the U.S. security apparatus, working under the control of the Patriot Act, could also "gather" research being conducted on such sensitive issues as terrorism, rogue states, or the drug trade. An article by journalist Caroline Alphonso, entitled "Universities Move to Hide Work from U.S. Eyes,"[24] cites the example that an "academic researching . . . nuclear weapons could find the work flagged by the Bush government."[25] Given the fact that President Barack Obama signed a proclamation in March 2010 stating that the Patriot Act will stand without changes for at least a year, we can assume that such covert intrusions will continue.

During 2006–2007, librarians, faculty, and students in Canada realized that, due to the Patriot Act, privacy related to campus activities and research interests was open to intrusion. As a result, many universities abandoned the U.S. server and created a Canadian equivalent at the University of Toronto where Canadian searches are now stored; however, that move may have been fruitless, given the anticipated revival of IP21C (or "lawful access" legislation) in Canada, which would, like the Patriot Act, make anybody's digital information available for government investigation.

In addition to research results, personal medical information of Canadian patients may also have been available to the U.S. Government. (Anton B. was pondering the potentially dangerous effects of distributing digitized health records in chapter 2.) The government of British Columbia outsourced the management of B.C. residents' medical records to a U.S. company whose servers were located in the United States. A 2004 report produced by the B.C. Information and Privacy Commissioner's Office, entitled "Privacy and the USA Patriot Act: Implications for British Columbia Public Sector Outsourcing,"[26] was a response to a lawsuit brought to the B.C. Supreme Court by the B.C. Government and Service Employees' Union. The union was concerned that B.C. Medical Services Plan records, if stored in the United

States, would be subject to Section 215 of the Patriot Act, which allows the FBI to conduct clandestine data-mining. The B.C. report poses two vital questions, both of which could be asked of equivalent U.S. healthcare privacy legislation and regulation:

1. The Patriot Act permits U.S. authorities to access personal information about British Columbians . . . through the outsourcing of public services, in the custody or under the control of U.S.-linked private sector providers. If it does, under what conditions can this occur?
2. What are the implications for public body compliance with the personal privacy protection of the Freedom of Information and Protection of Privacy Act (FIPPA)? What measures can be suggested to eliminate or appropriately mitigate privacy risks affecting compliance with FIPPA?

The issue was taken up by B.C. and Canadian federal privacy commissioners, as well as the Canadian Federal Government. As a result, the Treasury Board of Canada created an online response, entitled "Privacy Matters: The Federal Strategy to Address Concerns about the USA Patriot Act and Transborder Data Flows."[27] The report resolved that balancing privacy with security concerns is, indeed, difficult and that policy guidance between different parts of government will continue. But, once again, the introduction of Canada's potential equivalent to the Patriot Act, IP21C, may undermine any expectations of maintaining healthcare privacy in Canada.

Another example of the ways in which health information can be compromised occurred when 483 nonencrypted digitized health records were lost by a courier in 2007 and never retrieved. (In Canada, with its universal healthcare system, health records are routinely shared by provinces in which patients have taken advantage of another province's health services.) According to a 2008 report published by the National Union of Public and General Employees, the records included names, government healthcare identification numbers, ages, and sexes. Why the records were not encrypted or the information not disaggregated is unclear.

The Ontario Government's ongoing effort to digitize health records (known as the e-Health Initiative), became infamous in 2009 because of wild, untendered overspending. As a result, the project, scheduled to be completed by 2015, has attracted more attention in the press about graft and the delayed deployment of contracts than about privacy; however, one article published in the *Canadian Medical Association*

Journal noted that, while the provincial government had been shown to have wasted more than $1 billion, after seven years of planning, nothing had been done to revise privacy legislation to address electronic health records.[28] Despite Ontario's problems in implementing its electronic health record (EHR) plans, its efforts are part of national and international projects under way, due to the widely held belief that speed, connectivity, and (at least hoped for) security of records will improve healthcare and, moreover, diminish healthcare costs. All Canadian provinces and territories are developing their own EHR projects, some apparently more successfully than others, although they are all still works in progress.

What implications are there for EHRs in the United States, where the development of a national online personal health information system is also under way? As in the case of Canada, in the United States there are disparate state, local, and federal plans to implement EHR systems, all of which are subject to citizen and health professional concerns about security and privacy of patient records, as an article by Molly Merrill, entitled "Privacy Hindering EHR Progress, Say Researchers," indicates.[29] Surveys, interviews, and focus groups that include questions about privacy have been conducted and reported on in both Canada and the United States, reports that are addressed further in chapters 5 and 7.

In light of the RefWorks and healthcare records issues, it is clear that the B.C. privacy commissioner's concern for privacy welfare is well-founded in any country or jurisdiction; nevertheless, in certain narrowly defined circumstances, there can be potential benefits for disclosing health records electronically, or not, to responsible healthcare and security authorities, for reasons pointed out in chapter 7.

QUESTIONS FOR DISCUSSION

1. Do you agree with justices Warren and Brandeis when they argue that we have a right to "be let alone"? What is a right?
2. Why do "digital natives" give up so much of their personal information, even though they are warned about the possible negative consequences?
3. What did Mark Zuckerberg mean when he said that the "social norm [privacy] is just something that has evolved over time"?
4. Can we trust any big database with our personal information (for example, the U.S. Government, colleges, credit card companies, or hospitals with electronic health records)?

NOTES

1. Judith A. Swanson, *The Public and the Private in Aristotle's Political Philosophy* (Ithaca, NY: Cornell University Press, 1992).
2. Swanson, *The Public and the Private in Aristotle's Political Philosophy*, 8.
3. Hannah Arendt, *The Human Condition* (Chicago: University of Chicago Press, 1958).
4. Arendt, *The Human Condition*, 38.
5. Samuel D. Warren and Louis D. Brandeis, "The Right to Privacy." *Harvard Law Review* 4(5) (1890): 193–207.
6. Zuckerberg was being interviewed at the Crunchie Awards in San Francisco. The awards recognize advances in IT.
7. Warren and Brandeis, "The Right to Privacy," 193.
8. Warren and Brandeis, "The Right to Privacy," 193.
9. Daniel J. Solove, *The Future of Reputation: Gossip, Rumor, and Privacy on the Internet* (New Haven, CT: Yale University Press, 2007).
10. John Palfrey, *Born Digital: Understanding the First Generation of Digital Natives* (New York: Basic Books, 2008).
11. Patricia Sanchez Abril, "A (My) Space of One's Own: On Privacy and Online Social Networks." *Northwestern Journal of Technology and Intellectual Property* 6(1) (Fall 2007): 73–88.
12. The workforce at Research in Motion, the maker of the Blackberry, in Waterloo, Ontario, Canada, is 4,000. The city's population is 125,000, including almost 20,000 engineering and computer science students at the University of Waterloo.
13. Sanchez Abril, "A (My) Space of One's Own."
14. John Stuart Mill, *On Liberty and Utilitarianism* (New York: Borzoi, 1969). Economists refer to this concept as the "minimax principle," in which the most favorable decision among a number of choices is the one that would bring the least harm if something went wrong.
15. C. Arthur Van Lear Jr., "The Formation of Social Relationships: A Longitudinal Study of Social Penetration." *Human Communication Research* 13(3) (1987): 299–322.
16. Valerie Steeves, "The Next Generation Dragon: Children's Online Privacy." 29th International Conference of Data Protection and Privacy Commissioners, Montreal, Quebec, Canada, 2007.
17. See Carly Brandenburg, "The Newest Way to Screen Job Applicants: A Social Networker's Nightmare." *Federal Communications Law Journal* 60(3): 597–626.
18. The Conservatives are a right-of-center party, roughly equivalent to the Republican Party in their social and economic outlook.
19. Martin R. Dowding, "Terrorism, Trade, and Internet Privacy." *Canadian Journal of Communication* 30(1) (2005): 89–98.
20. "No-fly" lists were created by and are maintained by the Transportation Security Administration (TSA) and other federal intelligence agencies. The TSA is discussed further in chapter 5.

21. Until 9/11, Canada's military was largely known for its peacekeeping duties, usually carried out under the aegis of the United Nations. Since 9/11, Canadian forces have increasingly taken part in conflicts at the side of U.S. forces, especially in Afghanistan.

22. RefWorks, www.refworks.com.

23. The National Public Radio site explains the effect of Section 215 by saying, "The Patriot Act widened the government's surveillance powers in an effort to fight terrorism. But many contend it also put civil liberties at risk. Among the act's most controversial provisions is Section 215. It allows investigators broad access to library, bookstore, rental car, and many other records, and it prevents the recipient of such an order from disclosing the request for records."

24. Caroline Alphonso, "Universities Move to Hide Work from U.S. Eyes." *Globe and Mail*, November 11, 2006. Accessed from www.theglobeandmail.com/news/technology/article855078.ece.

25. Alphonso, "Universities Move to Hide Work from U.S. Eyes," 42.

26. British Columbia Information and Privacy Commissioner's Office, "Privacy and the USA Patriot Act: Implications for British Columbia Public Sector Outsourcing." Accessed from the Office of the Information Privacy Commissioner, www.llbc.leg.bc.ca/public/pubdocs/bcdocs/372251/summary2004.pdf.

27. Treasury Board of Canada, "Privacy Matters: The Federal Strategy to Address Concerns about the USA Patriot Act and Transborder Data Flows." Accessed from www.tbs-sct.gc.ca/pubs_pol/gospubs/tbm_128/pm-prp/pm-prp-eng.asp.

28. Paul Christopher Webster, "Ontario's Plan for Electronic Health Care Records Is at Risk, Official Says." *Canadian Medical Association Journal* 182(6) (2010): E233–E254.

29. M. Merrill, "Privacy Hindering EHR Progress, Say Researchers." *Healthcare IT News*, September 21, 2010. Accessed from www.healthcareitnews.com/print/18106.

4

Privacy Legislation and Policy: Illusory Protection?

Privacy has been recognized internationally as a separate human right[1] and enshrined in many national constitutions and declarations throughout the world; however, in relatively recent history, there is still a broad and complex variation in the way privacy issues are interpreted in different sectors in public and private situations, both within countries and across borders. The most cited reference to a universal fundamental right to privacy is in the United Nations Declaration of Human Rights (UNDHR), which states the following:

> No one shall be subjected to arbitrary interference with his privacy, family, home, or correspondence, nor to attacks upon his honor and reputation. Everyone has the right to the protection of the law against such interference or attacks.[2]

That would seem similar to the four principles set out by Privacy International (information, bodily, communications, and territorial privacy), but, like many other "declarations" the UNDHR is not "actionable" legislation. It is no more than an ethical, well-meaning framework designed to guide the creators of regulations, legislation, and policy. It is striking that privacy legislation negotiated by the United States, Canada, and other countries is a relatively recent idea. When Samuel D. Warren and Louis D. Brandeis finished their famous article with "the common law has always recognized a man's house as his castle,"[3] they were referring to law as it had been practiced (outside of the rule of legislation) beginning in England in the eleventh century, whereby judges considered historic legal cases to set precedents to guide later cases.[4]

U.S. PRIVACY LEGISLATION

U.S. privacy legislation began to develop in the late eighteenth century. After the United States won its independence from Britain, it began to define itself with its own laws, most particularly with the U.S. Constitution (1791, part of which is not unlike the 1948 UNDHR). Privacy in the United States is cited as having been codified in the Fourth Amendment of the U.S. Constitution, which states the following:

> The right of the people to be secure in their persons, houses, papers, and effects, against unreasonable searches and seizures, shall not be violated, and no Warrants shall issue, but upon probable cause, supported by Oath or affirmation, and particularly describing the place to be searched, and the persons or things to be seized.[5]

It was not until almost 200 years later that Canadian citizens had similar wording in their Charter of Rights and Freedoms (1982), representing a tentative departure from its colonial status. Section 7 of the Charter of Rights and Freedoms reads, "Everyone has the right to life, liberty, and security of the person and the right not to be deprived thereof except in accordance with the principles of fundamental justice," and Section 8 continues, "Everyone has the right to be secure against unreasonable search and seizure."[6]

In the United States, Federal Criminal Procedure Rules and Title 18 of the United States Code[7] refer to each other, as other state legislation does, to address the limited reference to privacy in the U.S. Constitution; however, the Fourth Amendment of the U.S. Constitution is considered the foundation for U.S. legislation and policy regarding the reasonableness of "search and seizure." What is striking about both the U.S. Constitution and the Canadian Charter of Rights and Freedoms is that what is "unreasonable" is not clearly defined. Consequently, a lack of clarification of what is "unreasonable" may lead to the infringement of a person's privacy.

The U.S. Privacy Act,[8] created to protect personal information held by the U.S. Federal Government, was not created until 1974 and, even then, according to Bennett and Raab,[9] it was stymied by resistance from the private sector's interest in overcoming the "information privacy" of consumers and different views held by the federal government and states' rights to create their own legislation.[10]

According to Lee Gomes,[11] the U.S. has "more than 300 privacy-related laws on the books, in both Washington, D.C., and state capitals." There are also countless corporate policies that Gomes comments on:

> On the one hand, laws designed to keep consumers apprised of privacy issues have resulted in a deluge of privacy notices, consent forms and security alerts into mailboxes, both real and electronic. You can't see a doctor, sign up for a bank account or visit a Web site without collecting your share of this paperwork. Rather than making people more private, though, the torrent of notifications leaves most of them so desensitized that they stop caring.[12]

Since the creation of the Privacy Act of 1974, many other U.S. laws have been created to address different corporate sectors and protect both children and adults. Some of the policies and laws regarding commerce are based on the legal powers of the U.S. Federal Trade Commission (FTC), the self-regulatory guidelines of the Safe Harbor Agreement, and Fair Information Practice Principles inherent in privacy legislation in the United States, Canada, and Europe. The Fair Information Practice Principles, as described by the FTC, have been developed over time and are based on roughly thirty years of cooperative deliberation among Canada, the United States, and Europe and have contributed to the creation of many other policies that regulate the collection and use of personal information.

The Fair Information Practice Principles are similar to the Canadian Standards Association's (CSA) *Model Code for the Protection of Personal Information* (published as an international code in 1996 and described later in this chapter; see appendix A for the CSA principles; see appendix B[13] for an example of a university privacy policy influenced, in part, by the CSA model and the Ontario, Canada, provincial Freedom of Information and Privacy Protection Act [FIPPA]; see also appendix B for the URL to access this legislation). The FTC principles, a full description of which can be found at the FTC website,[14] are outlined as follows, in a condensed form:

1. Notice/Awareness: This section describes the most "fundamental" principle—that a consumer can only make an informed choice about disclosing personal information if he or she is made familiar with an "entity's" policies on collection, use, and reuse of his or her information.
2. Choice/Consent: This core principle refers to the options a consumer has with regard to his or her information and whether he or she will allow it to be used for any purpose other than for which it was originally collected.

3. Access/Participation: This principle pertains to a person's having access to his or her personal information that has already been collected for the sake of knowing that it is accurate and to correct any errors.
4. Integrity/Security: This is directly related to the previous principle in that not only does it refer to accuracy but that, when accurate, a person's information is kept safe from other parties and is done so with both "managerial and technical" methods, such as encryption. This principle also refers to whether information is destroyed when it is no longer needed or it is put into a form that will no longer identify a person (e.g., through disaggregation of identifiable personal profiles).
5. Enforcement/Redress: This principle helps guarantee that, even if a privacy policy is part of a self-regulatory regime, there should be some sort of legislation to resolve consumers' complaints about their personal information being used improperly through "civil and criminal sanctions." This action should be carried out either by "private remedies" or, ultimately, "government enforcement."

The Fair Information Practice Principles, as described by the FTC, do not, however, specifically address the issue of information collected from children. Assuming that children do not possess the maturity to judge which and how much of their personal information should be put into the hands of marketers (and other parties), the FTC includes a separate section directed at parents in whose hands the responsibility to protect their children's privacy lies. Unlike Canada, which has no specific legislation regarding children's online safety, the United States created the Children's Online Privacy Protection Act[15] to protect children's information and communications privacy and security.

U.S. SAFE HARBOR AGREEMENT

The following is the U.S. rationale for the Safe Harbor Agreement, which helps confirm Bennett and Raab's observation that businesses resist mandatory privacy legislation:

> The European Commission's Directive on Data Protection went into effect in October 1998, and would prohibit the transfer of personal data to non-European Union nations that do not meet the European "adequacy" standard for privacy protection. While the United States and the European Union share the goal of enhancing privacy protec-

> tion for their citizens, the United States takes a different approach to privacy from that taken by the European Union. The United States uses a sectoral approach that relies on a mix of legislation, regulation, and *self-regulation*. The European Union, however, relies on comprehensive legislation that, for example, requires creation of government data protection agencies, registration of databases with those agencies, and, in some instances, prior approval before personal data processing may begin. As a result of these different privacy approaches, the Directive could have significantly hampered the ability of U.S. companies to engage in many trans-Atlantic transactions.
>
> To bridge these different privacy approaches and provide a streamlined means for U.S. organizations to comply with the Directive, the U.S. Department of Commerce, in consultation with the European Commission, developed a "safe harbor" framework. *The safe harbor, approved by the European Union in 2000, is an important way for U.S. companies to avoid experiencing interruptions in their business dealings with the European Union or facing prosecution by European authorities under European privacy laws.* Certifying to the safe harbor will assure that EU organizations know that your company provides "adequate" privacy protection, as defined by the Directive.[16] (emphasis added)

The measures taken by the United States, however, particularly the voluntary/self-regulatory Safe Harbor Agreement, are not as robust as steps taken in Canada (or European Union countries) and other member countries of the Organisation for Economic Co-operation and Development (OECD). According to the Media Awareness Network,

> America's Privacy Act of 1974 protects all records held by U.S. Federal Government agencies and requires them to apply basic fair information practices in the collection, storage, and use of personal information. But unlike Canada, which has the Office of the Privacy Commissioner, the United States has no independent agency to oversee privacy issues.[17]

Making contemporary international privacy law and policy has been obviously contentious in light of some of the differences cited above. The OECD was one of the earliest bodies to develop an information policy (and a method for creating policies, the OECD Privacy Statement Generator)[18] that addresses personal privacy internationally. *Guidelines on the Protection of Privacy and Transborder Flows of Personal Data,*[19] which affects both Canada and, to a lesser extent, the United States (as its protectionist laws suggest), as OECD members, was designed to "harmonize national privacy legislation and provide a framework for facilitating international flows of data."[20]

As Bennett and Raab point out, the contention was due partly to European fears that the U.S. espousal of the principle that information flows should rarely be impeded was a veiled attempt to protect U.S. hegemony in the marketplace. Some Americans, on the other hand, saw ulterior trade-protectionist motivations behind the data-protection label.[21]

CANADIAN LEGISLATION AND POLICY

While there are many laws, regulations, and policies that affect public and private sector activities, there are two federal privacy laws in Canada, the Privacy Act of 1983 and the Personal Information Protection and Electronic Documents Act (PIPEDA) of 2000. The Privacy Act, much like its U.S. equivalent, applies to federal government departments and other federal bodies by limiting the collection, use, and disclosure of personal information held by those bodies. The act permits Canadian citizens to access their personal information and correct anything they consider—or can prove to be—incorrect.

PIPEDA, on the other hand, applies to the private sector by controlling the way in which companies collect, use, disclose, and dispose of personal information. The commercial bodies covered by PIPEDA primarily include banks; the telecommunications, publishing, and service industries; and certain institutions and corporations regulated by federal, provincial, or territorial legislation. In some circumstances, however, the federal government may exempt some provinces and territories that have privacy legislation that is deemed similar to the federal acts.

Overseeing all privacy acts in Canada and infractions against them is the Office of the Privacy Commissioner and equivalent commissioners or ombudspersons in the provinces and territories, all of whom act on behalf of persons whose privacy has been deemed to have been breached by persons, corporations, or government. The United States has no equivalent entity.[22]

When we *willingly* (or are compelled to) submit our personal information to any public or private institution, most of us hope that the information will remain confidential and be handled according to "fair information principles," similar to the FTC's aforementioned principles. The widely respected CSA *Model Code for the Protection of Personal Information*, designed to help control the collection, use, and disclosure of personal data, is inherent in many voluntary principles and policies. The model's influence is apparent in the fact that it is appended to PIPEDA. Those organizations that follow the model and PIPEDA can prevent personal data from falling into the hands of third, fourth, or fifth parties that might overwhelm consumers with advertisements, sales pitches, or charity appeals. These practices can also help to prevent misuse of financial information or identity theft.

According to the CSA, both individuals and organizations can be confident that their interests can be protected by following the code:

> The global information age offers huge economic and personal benefits. At the same time, it raises concerns about the individual's right to privacy and the protection of personal data. The CSA's *Model Code for the Protection of Personal Information* (Q830) sets out ten principles that balance the privacy rights of individuals and the information requirements of private organizations.
>
> The Privacy Code was developed using the CSA's renowned consensus-based methods. Drawing on the experience gained through this development process, the CSA has published a suite of companion resources to help an organization put the code into practice, wherever business is carried out in the world today. In Canada, the key elements of the Privacy Code are now incorporated into the Personal Information Protection and Electronic Documents Act (PIPEDA). All organizations that comply with the CSA standard can be confident that they meet the federal requirements of PIPEDA. All organizations involved in multinational exchanges of information can also be confident that they are addressing increasingly rigorous international demands for the protection of personal information.[23]

The CSA published its own guide to the code, *Making the CSA Privacy Code Work for You*,[24] which explains how to apply the code's principles when an organization wants to create a transparent, understandable privacy policy. The guide also explains how an organization can "self-declare" that it has adopted the code and how it can "verify" its compliance by submitting its policy to CSA (and becoming subject to a privacy policy audit). When the policy is "registered" with the CSA for further recognition of its standards, it is subject to a further audit.

Is the Privacy Code Adequate?

Despite the CSA's positive defense, at least one author suggests that our trust in the Privacy Code be limited, for a number of reasons. The first problem is that adopting the code is voluntary. No company or organization *must* use the code. Six years after the code was introduced, Philippa Lawson, then a lawyer for the Public Interest Advocacy

Centre, in Ottawa, made the following observations about flaws in the code:

> It has become clear that some important aspects of the code are subject to widely differing interpretation. The vagueness of some provisions leaves both businesses and consumers uncertain as to their proper meaning and application and encourages each interested party to interpret the provision to their advantage. The result is marketplace confusion, increased business expense, reduced utility of the code, and loss of confidence by consumers in the protections that the code was meant to afford.[25]

Despite the overall trust and faith in the code, the vagueness and differing interpretations referred to by Lawson are not the only problems. Each institution, corporation, and government body also has to determine which policy, regulation, or law applies to it and how to comply. In both Canada and the United States, the complex matrix of local, regional, national, and international law and policies raises such barriers for all concerned. Creating policies and legislation at any level is always a challenge. On the one hand, doing so provides the opportunity to appear (and perhaps even be) responsible. But on the other hand, it allows policymakers to take advantage of a public that doesn't understand policy language or care to read complex, vague, or lengthy policies.

In "Nobody Reads Your Privacy Notice? It's Time for a New One!"[26] Susan E. Gindin refers to the often-cited case of Sears Holdings Management Corp. (Sears), the privacy policy of which was deemed "deceptive" under the Federal Trade Commission Act. Sears advertised a software package for shoppers to become part of Sears "community" that, unbeknownst to shoppers, tracked their financial and medical histories. That tracking was barely mentioned, except in an additional (significantly *combined*) privacy statement/user license agreement, which made it clear to potential users that if they did not sign the agreement they could not be part of the "community" of other users whose consent had, presumably, been acquired.

Similar corporate misbehavior (mischief or carelessness) with consumer information is rampant. Other examples of such misuse are more fully explored in chapter 8, which concentrates on social networking.

PRIVACY POLICIES: WHO READS THEM?

Privacy policies have sprung up on virtually every site on the Web. We willingly *submit* our personal data to the sites, or have it recorded by "cookies," the nefarious files stored on computers that are accessed by Web servers to create a "profile" of a person's searches. Companies and services claim to "guarantee" the security of their sites and assert that our personal statistics or credit card information are encrypted or made secure in some other manner. Many of those corporations have crafted their policies with the assistance of such groups as the CSA or OECD and, consequently, consider themselves to be, or appear to be, trustworthy. But, as Lawson suggests, because policies have been adopted or adapted according to specific situations, they are not always consistent or clear enough to be understood. It should also be noted that clarity is often lost in the sheer length of a policy, as in the case of Facebook.

According to the *New York Times*,[27] Facebook's privacy policy has grown from 1,004 words in 2005 to 5,830 words in 2010, and it is now longer than the U.S. Constitution, which contains 4,543 words. In "Facebook Privacy: A Bewildering Tangle of Options," we also learn that its "Privacy FAQ" page is 45,000 words, the equivalent of roughly 150 pages. We also learn that, despite a user having changed his or her privacy settings, as of May 2010, "friends" shared the user's "name, profile, picture, gender, and more with third-party websites and applications,"[28] without the user's or friend's knowledge.

PRIVACY POLICIES AND LAWS AT "HOME"

Quite the opposite of Facebook's ever-widening *access to everyone* is the notion that we, in some circumstances, can actually ask to "be let alone." The U.S. and Canadian governments have provided millions of home phone, cell phone, Voice over Internet Protocol, fax, and telephone typewriter users with a version of a right to privacy. The U.S. National Do Not Call Registry,[29] enacted in 2003, was developed by the Federal Communications Commission and FTC. The Canadian National Do Not Call List,[30] enacted in 2009, is overseen by the Canadian Radio-Television and Telecommunications Commission (CRTC). Both lists were created to protect consumers from being inundated by telemarketers and perpetrators of telephone fraud. Telemarketers were not very enthusiastic and foresaw the loss of millions of jobs. In both countries, however, several exemptions are allowed, including ongoing business relationships, newspapers looking for subscribers, political party representatives, and registered charities. The lists also help commercial enterprises know whom not to call, so that they will not be fined.

According to the FTC, the U.S. effort has been a great success, having resulted in penalties of $85 million and more than $325 million in consumer redress payments. Canada, on the other hand, had not pursued many violators, until late in 2010. A July 2010 Canadian Broadcasting Corporation report[31] showed that only $250 had been collected, out of a total of $73,000 in fines; however, in December 2010, Xentel DM, a telemarketing firm, paid a record Cdn. $500,000 after the CRTC fined it for calling numbers on the National Do Not Call List.

WHAT COMES OUT: DO WE THROW OUT OUR PRIVACY WITH THE TRASH?

Apparently, yes, we do throw out our privacy with the trash. If a "man's house is his castle," then what comes out of his (or her) castle in the form of garbage may not be subject to territorial, communications, and information privacy. Two legal cases, one in Canada and one in the United States, point to the fact that once our garbage is outside of our homes, we lose our right against "unreasonable search and seizure." A frequently cited case occurred in California in 1988, when the U.S. Supreme Court (based on the U.S. Constitution) said that "police may search a person's curbside garbage without a warrant, because individuals do not have an expectation of privacy in the garbage they put outside for collection";[32] however, a number of U.S. states have argued that a warrant is necessary.

In reference to a 2009 decision of the Canadian Supreme Court, lawyer David T. S. Fraser posted the following on the Canadian Privacy Law Blog:

> If you throw something out into the garbage, it is hard to say you've not abandoned it. You've given it up. . . . It really is a bit of a stretch to say that you expect something you put in your trash will remain confidential in most cases.[33]

Both cases point to the issue of being spied on, the subject of chapter 5.

QUESTIONS FOR DISCUSSION

1. Of the institutions presented in this chapter, which group(s) do you feel have the most positive input into guaranteeing our personal privacy?
2. What is the meaning of the Fourth Amendment of the U.S. Constitution?

3. With the Fourth Amendment of the U.S. Constitution and Sections 7 and 8 of Canada's Charter of Rights and Freedoms in mind, what do you think "reasonable" search and seizure might be?
4. Are "self-regulatory" measures adequate in guaranteeing our privacy?
5. What are the strongest and weakest points of privacy policies?

NOTES

1. United Nations Declaration of Human Rights (1948, Article 12). The United Nations International Covenant on Civil and Political Rights (1966, Article 17) articulates the same principles.

2. UNDHR (1948, Article 12).

3. Samuel D. Warren and Louis D. Brandeis, "The Right to Privacy." *Harvard Law Review* 4(5) (1890): 193. The English jurist Sir Edward Coke (1552–1634) was quoted as saying, "[F]or a man's house is his castle . . . for where shall a man be safe, if it not be in his house?" Cited in Amanda Vickery, "An Englishman's Home Is His Castle?: Thresholds, Boundaries, and Privacies in the Eighteenth-Century London House." *Past and Present* 199(1) (2008): 154, note 12.

4. In the United States, the only state that does not follow common law is Louisiana. In Canada, Quebec is the only province that does not follow it. They are both "civil code" jurisdictions, which derives from their historic connections to France.

5. U.S. Constitution Online, "Amendment 4, Search and Seizure." Accessed from www.usconstitution.net/xconst_Am4.html.

6. Canadian Charter of Rights and Freedoms Online, "Part 1 of the Constitution Act, 1982." Accessed from www.laws.justice.gc.ca/en/charter/.

7. The United States Code is the codification by subject matter of the general and permanent laws of the United States. It is divided by broad subjects into fifty titles and published by the Office of the Law Revision Counsel of the U.S. House of Representatives. (Title 18 refers to electronic communications privacy.) See www.gpoaccess.gov/uscode/.

8. The U.S. Department of Justice website describes the act by saying, "The Privacy Act of 1974, 5 U.S.C. § 552a, establishes a code of *fair information practices* that governs the collection, maintenance, use, and dissemination of personally identifiable information about individuals that is maintained in systems of records by federal agencies." Accessed from www.justice.gov/opcl/privacyact1974.htm.

9. Colin J. Bennett and Charles D. Raab, *The Governance of Privacy: Policy Instruments in Global Perspective* (Cambridge, MA: MIT Press, 2006).

10. Bennett and Raab, *The Governance of Privacy*, 131.

11. Lee Gomes, "Privacy Perils." *Forbes* 183(11): 34–37.

12. Gomes, "Privacy Perils," 34.
13. Appendix B is Wilfrid Laurier University's privacy coordinator's website, which is included to provide the opportunity to analyze a privacy policy by using the CSA model code and other principles introduced throughout this book.
14. Federal Trade Commission, "Fair Information Practice Principles." Accessed from www.ftc.gov/reports/privacy3/fairinfo.shtm.
15. Children's Online Privacy Protection Act of 1998, "Title XIII: Children's Online Privacy Protection." Accessed from www.ftc.gov/ogc/coppa1.htm.
16. Export.gov, "U.S.-EU Safe Harbor Overview." Accessed from www.export.gov/safeharbor/eu/eg_main_018476.asp.
17. Media Awareness Network, "Information Privacy: U.S. Legislation." Accessed from www.media-awareness.ca/english/issues/privacy/us_legislation_privacy.cfm.
18. See the "OECD Privacy Statement Generator," available at www.oecd.org/sti/privacygenerator.
19. Organisation for Economic Co-operation and Development, *Guidelines on the Protection of Privacy and Transborder Flows of Personal Data*. Accessed from www.oecd.org/document/18/0,3343,en_2649_34255_1815186_1_1_1_1,00.html.
20. Bennett and Raab, *The Governance of Privacy*, 88.
21. Bennett and Raab, *The Governance of Privacy*, 88.
22. There are, however, privacy officers in California and Hawaii and in a variety of federal offices, including the Department of Homeland Security and FTC.
23. Canadian Standards Association, "Privacy Code." Accessed from www.csa.ca/cm/ca/en/privacy-code.
24. Canadian Standards Association, *Making the CSA Privacy Code Work for You* (Etobicoke, Ontario, Canada: Canadian Standards Association, 1996).
25. Philippa Lawson, "PIAC Comments on CSA Privacy Code." October 20, 2002. Accessed from www.piac.ca/privacy/piac_comments_on_csa_privacy_code.
26. Susan E. Gindin, "Nobody Reads Your Privacy Notice? It's Time for a New One!" Accessed from www.info-law.com/nobodyreads.html.
27. Gilbert Gates, "Facebook Privacy: A Bewildering Tangle of Options." *New York Times*, May 12, 2010. Accessed from www.nytimes.com/interactive/2010/05/12/business/facebook-privacy.html.
28. Gates, "Facebook Privacy: A Bewildering Tangle of Options."
29. See the U.S. National Do Not Call Registry at www.ftc.gov/donotcall.
30. See Canada's Do Not Call List home page at www.lnnte-dncl.gc.ca/index-eng.
31. Canadian Broadcasting Corporation News, "U.S. Do Not Call List Puts Canada's to Shame." July 13, 2010. Accessed from www.cbc.ca/consumer/story/2010/07/13/con-do-not-call.html.
32. Kevin M. Keenan, *Invasion of Privacy* (Santa Barbara, CA: ABC-CLIO, 2005), 176.
33. David T. S. Fraser, Canadian Privacy Law Blog, "Mind Your Trash." Accessed from http://blog.privacylawyer.ca.

5

Surveillance: Privacy Denied

Despite the legislation and policy efforts discussed in chapter 4, for many privacy only remains an illusion. Consider the experiences encountered by Anton B. (as "everyman") in chapter 2. Anton B.'s every move is recorded and his purchases are logged, and his son's school activities are available to be watched through a spy camera. A record of Anton B.'s entire medical information is kept on a single chip. His computer keystrokes at work are counted. His phone and Internet correspondence are observed and stored. His face and body are scrutinized by the newest x-ray technology, as are travelers at airports and "sensitive" government buildings. In short, his (and anyone else's) information privacy, bodily privacy, privacy of communications, and territorial privacy are all compromised in today's digital world.

But why should it be this way? Or, why should we *want* it to be this way? Some of the information collected about a person helps determine his or her consumer preferences, which is annoying but considered fair enough in a capitalist society; however, as the U.S. Federal Trade Commission's Fair Information Practice Principles and the Canadian Standards Association's *Model Code for the Protection of Personal Information* show, some information collection techniques may be questionable if the subject whose information is collected does not know why (or if) the information is collected or how it will be used once it is gathered. Some information is amassed to control traffic or the way people drive. Some information is collected for security, as in the case of information collected that "guarantees" our safety when we travel by air; however, in the narrative about Anton B.'s not-so-private day, it is unclear why there was so much workplace surveillance (the question of which is addressed more closely in chapter 6). But, given the fallout from September 11, 2001, and the ongoing "war on terror" and "war on drugs," Anton B.'s bodily and communications privacy are fair game, according to "experts" and citizens confident that their information is secure once it is collected. They are comfortable that surveillance, for the sake of presumed security, trumps privacy.

The surveillance just described and in Anton B.'s story is an example of what Michel Foucault[1] (following Jeremy Bentham's model[2]) calls the "panopticon," the "utopian" ideal of a physical, three-dimensional prisonlike structure (or, in Foucault's interpretation, a political power formulation) that allows the "governor" (or Orwell's "Big Brother," or whoever is in power) to watch everyone's behavior, all the time (or, at least to impel people to feel as though they are being watched). As Kirstie Ball and Frank Webster explain,

> Michel Foucault . . . took the panopticon as a central motif for modernity itself, adding that self-monitoring accompanies panopticism, with the inspected continuously feeling that they are subject to surveillance. Moreover, to Foucault, the panopticon is more than a physical place, since it now entails new "disciplines of order." . . . In the Foucaultian view, when surveillance is accompanied by such technologies as computerized tills and video cameras, then we have entered an era of the panopticon without walls.[3]

In other words, as Robert O'Harrow Jr.'s book title[4] and his references to the panopticon suggest, we may certainly feel as though there is "no place to hide."[5] The "panopticon without walls" describes the ideal behind U.S. and international surveillance techniques and legislation that have increased and intensified during the past ten or more years (or roughly since 9/11). Not long after 9/11, a number of efforts designed for computer "data-mining" (undetectable electronic snooping) were undertaken to seek out terrorists in the United States and internationally under the auspices of the Information Awareness Office, a suboffice of the U.S. Defense Advanced Research Projects Agency (DARPA).[6] No one really knows how many data-mining projects were under development or came to fruition; however, in 2004 the U.S. General Accounting Office (an investigative body that reports to Congress, much as the Auditor General does in Canada) reported that almost 200 projects were under way, more than half of which were "designed to collect and analyze large amounts of personal data about individuals to predict their behavior. Since the General Accounting Office excluded most of the classified [that is, "secret"] projects, the actual numbers would likely have been far higher."[7] One project that became public, however, was the ominously named Total Information Awareness program (TIA, later called Terrorism Information Awareness) that was to be implemented in 2002. Called a "vast electronic dragnet" in the *New York Times*, the TIA was defended by its director, Vice Admiral John M. Poindexter, in the following way:

> We must become much more efficient and more clever in the ways we find new sources of data, mine information from the new and old, generate information, make it available for analysis, convert it to knowledge, and create actionable options.[8]

Among other "sources of data" Poindexter referred to was e-mail in the United States.[9] Noting that the project would amount to a "system of national surveillance of the American public," the director of the Electronic Privacy Information Center (EPIC), Marc Rotenberg, said that it "could be the perfect storm for civil liberties in America."[10] Rotenberg's response was shared by enough senators and members of Congress that TIA was denied funding and died—as TIA, that is. Several years later, the Electronic Frontier Foundation, another U.S. digital rights group in line with EPIC, put forward a class-action suit accusing the telecommunications company AT&T of providing its telephone and Internet records to the impenetrable National Security Agency (NSA), which James Bamford wrote about in his book *The Shadow Factory: The Ultra-Secret NSA from 9/11 to the Eavesdropping of America*.[11]

Another law proposed soon after 9/11 was the Terrorism Information Prevention System, which would have required U.S. citizens to spy on each other in the style of the East German "Stasi" secret police program. Essentially, anyone could have snitched on his or her neighbor if they thought there was something suspicious about them. That proposal did not become law, again because of civil liberties concerns (among the left, the right, and libertarians), but also because such programs are notorious for false reports, as some neighbors simply don't like each other.[12]

Other laws, which remain active, include the USA Patriot Act and the European Union cybercrime law (which predated the Patriot Act). As pointed out in chapter 3, President Barack Obama signed a proclamation in March 2010, allowing the entire Patriot Act, including the draconian Section 215, to stand without changes for at least a year. It remains to be seen whether he will continue to support the law, but given the ongoing (or potentially permanent) "war on terror," it would not be surprising if he, or his successors, do so.

At the time of this writing, the Conservative Canadian Government had reintroduced (but not passed) "lawful access" legislation entitled Investigative Powers for the 21st Century (IP21C). That followed earlier efforts by the former Liberal Canadian Government to create a surveillance society in light of or under pressure from other international efforts, particularly in the United States. If IP21C, or its new equivalent, is true to its original intent, it would, like the recently revised and ongoing Communications Assistance for Law Enforcement Act (CALEA) of 1994, demand that Internet service providers (ISPs) be prepared to surrender to security officials subscribers' personal information, without clear justification, and without anyone necessarily knowing that he or she is under suspicion or why. IP21C would also likely require ISPs to preserve data that users have saved on their systems, but for how long, in what format, and at what cost is unclear.

Canadians have been subject to such U.S. laws as the Patriot Act due to cross-border information storage outsourcing or intentional transborder flows of information by the Canadian Government (for such purposes as banking, trade, or international law), "no-fly" lists, and so on. But, in the post-9/11 era of paranoia, how much privacy is the U.S., Canadian, or any other government willing to take away to attempt to guarantee security? The U.S. security apparatus impinges on Canadians daily (and Mexicans as well, but that is another story), either at the border, within the United States, or even in Canada if Canadian information is held in U.S. databases. The effect of the U.S. surveillance apparatus (and similar laws put in place by other countries) is proving that great vigilance is required to maintain privacy, if we can expect it to be maintained at all.

However, as Peter Shields explains in "The Escalation of Telecommunications Surveillance,"[13] U.S. law enforcement was already ramping up electronic eavesdropping techniques prior to 9/11, in the 1990s. In a tradition virtually as old as electricity itself, wiretapping—originally literally "tapping" a wire to "feel" a message—has been a common procedure since the telegraph was invented in the 1830s. Wiretapping was used for the telephone by law enforcement as early as the 1890s (by then, "listening in" on a conversation, or "bugging") and was formally recognized and controlled in the United States by the Communications Act of 1934.

Many subsequent changes and new laws to allow electronic surveillance have been made since then, including the previously mentioned CALEA, the first act that not only promotes eavesdropping as a policy but also makes "clear a telecommunications carrier's *duty to cooperate* in the interception of communications for law enforcement purposes, and for other purposes"[14] (emphasis added) and to "engineer their networks and services so that law enforcement can continue to wiretap."[15]

SURVEILLANCE ON HOLIDAY

When I returned from holiday in another country to Canada not long ago via the United States, I was surprised to find that my luggage had been searched despite the fact that I had not stopped in the United States, except to change flights. I knew that my luggage had been searched because of the "Notice of Baggage Inspection" that was on top of my belongings when I opened my bags upon arriving home. The notice, from the Department of Homeland Security/Transportation Security Administration (see appendix D), said, "To protect you and your fellow passengers, the Transportation Security Administration is required by law to inspect all baggage." The immediate question was, why inspect me? Do all of my fellow passengers suspect me? Should I suspect everyone else?

While simply having one's baggage searched is intimidating, it is nothing compared to the increasingly sophisticated technical methods created for air travel to counter terrorism and stop drug trafficking, gun-running, and the transportation of other dangerous and illegal cargo. While there have been x-ray machines at airport check-in counters since the 1970s,[16] due to a series of hijackings, the most recent technology has an already paranoid public and panicked security apparatus at loggerheads. The use of "imaging technology," as the new body scanners are called, puts front and center the balance between security and privacy. As Lee Ferran[17] points out,

> While the [U.S.] Constitution protects people from "unreasonable searches," some experts are debating where to draw the line. The [body scanning] devices are designed to pick up illicit and potentially dangerous materials, but they also show private details of a traveler's body, such as breast implants or prosthetic devices.[18]

Such sentiment did not deter authorities from defending the technology. When Stewart Baker, a former Department of Homeland Security official, was interviewed about the issue he stated, "Given the choice between losing my privacy, some of it, and losing my life or losing someone I love, I'm going to choose to lose some privacy."[19] His response is problematic, especially since this latest technology is only one in a long line of techniques, each of which is causing us to "lose *some* privacy" each time we are subject to surveillance. It should cause us to wonder when we know we have lost it all. It should also cause us to ponder the value of the fundamental questions inherent in the Organisation for Economic Co-operation and Development's *Guidelines on the Protection of Privacy and Transborder Flows of Personal Data*, the Canadian Standards Association's *Model Code for the Protection of Personal Information*, and the U.S. Federal Trade Commission's Fair Information Practice Principles, which include the following: How, exactly, is the information being collected? For what reason is it collected? How long will it be held? What will ultimately happen to it?

SURVEILLANCE AT HOME AND SCHOOL

In a less universal but even more intrusive example of surveillance by "authorities," a case of completely unwarranted eavesdropping came to light in 2010 in a school district outside of Philadelphia, Pennsylvania. In what the Lower Merion School District claimed to be an effort to locate stolen or lost laptop computers, school officials activated Web cameras on computers loaned to students, regardless of where they were (even in students' bedrooms), regardless of whether the computer was reported lost or not. An investigation was carried out by the FBI and local police. The case went to the courts after a family discovered that their son had been photographed while asleep at home, and it was determined that staff of the school district's information technology department had taken at least 50,000 photographs.

PC Magazine columnist John C. Dvorak responded to the controversy with a brief but pithy warning about the ethics of the school's behavior. Dvorak closed his article "Society of Surveillance"[20] by saying, "My advice to people using loaned computers like this is to always assume that there is some sort of spyware planted. . . . Just assume you're being watched and heard, because you probably are."[21] This is a fitting introduction to the next section of this chapter about closed-circuit TV.

CLOSED-CIRCUIT TV

Like the panopticon, closed-circuit TV (CCTV) is meant to be, or appear to be, all-pervasive and all-seeing. After all, cameras appear to be everywhere, given the school laptop example, or, as Reginald Whitaker points out in *The End of Privacy: How Total Surveillance Is Becom-*

ing a Reality,[22] that a range of techniques from "nannycams" to face recognition technology are destroying privacy.

We are constantly reminded that we are being watched by public signs that read "These Premises Are under Video Surveillance." Virtually all of the public areas on university campuses, for example, are covered by CCTV. But what are the real effects? As citizens in public, when we see the cameras and know that we are being watched, as Dvorak suggests (like the panopticon example), do we control or change our behavior? Or, as many studies show, do we try to stay out of the camera's eye? Criminal behavior is known to change when cameras are present in that they "displace" crime. A large literature, much of it emanating from Britain, a country with one of the highest uses of CCTV in the world, shows that criminals frequently move to other areas to commit their crimes or change their criminal habits by being less conspicuous. The British think tank Privacy International (PI), which developed the four types of privacy intervention introduced in chapter 1, succinctly describes what CCTV is, what kinds of technologies are necessary, whether CCTV reduces crime, and what the public thinks of it.[23] PI cites an ABC *20/20* television interview with a senior Scottish police constable, Leslie Sharp, known for his strident defense of CCTV. In the interview, Sharp says the following:

> Certainly, the crime goes somewhere. I don't believe that just because you've got cameras in a city center that everyone says, "Oh well, we're going to give up crime and get a job." . . . We will gradually drive the criminal further away, and eventually, I hope to drive them into the sea.[24]

But not everyone is as serious about the supposed "benefits" of CCTV, as Colin J. Bennett points out in his book *The Privacy Advocates: Resisting the Spread of Surveillance*.[25] Bennett emphasizes that his book is "about those individuals and groups that have emerged from civil society [to object to surveillance] spontaneously and without official sanction, rather than about those within the state or the market."[26] One such group is the Surveillance Camera Players,[27] who, in the tradition of "guerrilla theater,"[28] oppose the use of CCTV. Their project, which began in New York City in 1996, involves the presentation of plays and skits in front of CCTV cameras to register their contempt and "entertain" those watching the screens. They came together as amateurs in an attempt to point out that, in their eyes, the "commodity" of public space is controlled by corporate police-state surveillance (that is, there really isn't a truly "public sphere" any longer).[29] At the same time, they say the following, somewhat tongue-in-cheek:

> The Surveillance Camera Players are just a bunch of Joes and Josephines who appreciate how boring it must be for law enforcement officers to watch the video images constantly being displayed on the closed-circuit TV surveillance systems. . . . The only time these officers have fun watching these monitors is when something illegal is going on. . . . The opportunity is to get those law enforcement officials watching something on television that isn't all sex and violence, and the problem is that a bored surveillant is an unattentive surveillant, and an unattentive surveillant is a waste of space, time, and money.[30]

Apart from a brief allusion to Anton B.'s experience as an employee, this chapter has largely referred to expectations of privacy (or the "right to be let alone") in public spaces. The next chapter addresses the precarious privacy threshold we cross when we enter the workplace.

QUESTIONS FOR DISCUSSION

1. Do you think the post-9/11 U.S. surveillance apparatus has gone too far?
2. Are the U.S. "no-fly" lists a good idea? Who does and does not benefit from them?
3. Should we worry about our mail, phone calls, e-mail, and Facebook, MySpace, and Twitter accounts being "overheard" by the U.S. Federal Government?
4. Do you agree with Stewart Baker, who said, "Given the choice between losing my privacy, some of it, and losing my life or losing someone I love, I'm going to choose to lose some privacy"?
5. Do you approve of CCTV?

NOTES

1. Michel Foucault, *Discipline and Punish: The Birth of the Prison*. Trans. Alan Sheridan (New York: Vintage Books, 1995).
2. Jeremy Bentham, *The Panopticon Writings* (London: Verso, 1995).
3. Kirstie Ball and Frank Webster, eds., *The Intensification of Surveillance: Crime, Terrorism, and Warfare in the Information Age* (London: Pluto Books, 2003), 6. See also David Lyon, *The Electronic Eye: The Rise of Surveillance Society* (Minneapolis: University of Minnesota Press, 1994).
4. Robert O'Harrow Jr., *No Place to Hide* (New York: Free Press, 2005).

5. Perhaps not so coincidentally, Robert O'Harrow Jr.'s title is the same as that of David Bradley's *No Place to Hide* (Boston: Little Brown, 1948), which warns of the universal, ubiquitous effect of radiation fallout from the atomic bomb.

6. DARPA invented the Internet in the 1970s.

7. Mark Williams, "The Total Information Awareness Project Lives On." *MIT Technology Review*, April 26, 2006. Accessed from www.technologyreview.com/read_article.aspx?ch=specialsection&sc=security&id=16741.

8. Quoted by John Markoff in "Pentagon Plans a Computer System That Would Peek at Personal Data of Americans." *New York Times*, November 9, 2002. Accessed from www.nytimes.com/2002/11/09/politics/09COMP.html.

9. Poindexter was already well-known to the American public as a co-conspirator in the complex Iran-Contra Affair, for which he was charged with a felony for making illegal and secret arms deals with Iran and supporting ultra-right-wing Nicaraguan death squads during the Reagan administration.

10. Quoted by John Markoff in "Pentagon Plans a Computer System That Would Peek at Personal Data of Americans."

11. James Bamford, *The Shadow Factory: The Ultra-Secret NSA from 9/11 to the Eavesdropping of America* (New York: Doubleday, 2008).

12. See, for example, Ritt Goldstein, "United States Planning to Recruit Americans as Citizen Spies." July 15, 2002. Accessed from www.smh.com.au/articles/2002/07/14/1026185141232.html. See also Brian Doherty, "An American Stasi." July 16, 2002. Accessed from http://reason.com/archives/2002/07/16/an-american-stasi.

13. Peter Shields, "The Escalation of Telecommunications Surveillance." *Peace Review* 14(3) (2002): 325–30.

14. Ask CALEA, "Communications Assistance for Law Enforcement Act of 1994," Title 1, Section 101, paragraph 1. Accessed from www.askcalea.net/calea.

15. Shields, "The Escalation of Telecommunications Surveillance," 325.

16. Emily Harwood, "Airport Security." May 1, 1997. Accessed from http://securitysolutions.com/mag/security_airport_security/.

17. Lee Ferran, "Delicate Balance: Airline Security vs. Personal Privacy: Imaging Technology Could Make Passengers Safer, but at What Cost?" Accessed from http://abcnews.go.com/print?id=9439705.

18. Ferran, "Delicate Balance: Airline Security vs. Personal Privacy," n.p.

19. Ferran, "Delicate Balance: Airline Security vs. Personal Privacy," n.p.

20. John C. Dvorak, "Society of Surveillance." *PC Magazine*, June 1, 2010. Accessed from www.pcmag.com/article2/0,2817,2364473,00.asp.

21. Dvorak, "Society of Surveillance," n.p.

22. Reginald Whitaker, *The End of Privacy: How Total Surveillance Is Becoming a Reality* (New York: New Press, 1999). See, especially, chapter 4, "The Night Has a Thousand Eyes: New Technologies of Surveillance."

23. Privacy International, "CCTV Frequently Asked Questions." Accessed from www.privacyinternational.org/article.shtml?cmd%5B347%5D=x-347-61925.

24. Privacy International, "CCTV Frequently Asked Questions," n.p.

25. Colin J. Bennett, *The Privacy Advocates: Resisting the Spread of Surveillance* (Cambridge, MA: MIT Press, 2008).
26. Bennett, *The Privacy Advocates*, ix.
27. Surveillance Camera Players, *We Know You Are Watching* (New York: Factory School, 2006).
28. YourDictionary.com defines guerrilla theater as a "form of propaganda or political protest in which a group of activists perform satirical skits, sing songs, engage in playful pranks, and so forth, in the midst of a public event or activity." Accessed from www.yourdictionary.com/guerrilla-theater.
29. See Jürgen Habermas, *The Structural Transformation of the Public Sphere: An Inquiry into a Category of Bourgeois Society* (Cambridge, MA: MIT Press, 1991).
30. Surveillance Camera Players, *We Know You Are Watching*, n.p.

6

Privacy in the Workplace

Privacy has different purposes and functions in the world of business that should balance ethical and legal relations among employers, employees, and customers. On one hand, a company wants to be trusted by its customers for its compliance with legislation, fairness, and good sense. On the other hand, a company wants to be trusted by its employees for its compliance with legislation and policies in the workplace and develop appropriate and fair power relations.[1] Depending on the type of workplace, all of Privacy International's (PI) categories, including information, bodily, communications, and territorial privacy, introduced in chapter 1, can come into play.

RELATIONS WITH CUSTOMERS

In keeping with the Canadian Standards Association's (CSA) *Model Code for the Protection of Personal Information* or similar sets of principles, such as the Organisation for Economic Co-operation and Development's *Guidelines on the Protection of Privacy and Transborder Flows of Personal Data* or the Federal Trade Commission's Fair Information Practice Principles, it is a business's responsibility to keep the information it collects from customers secure to avoid identity theft caused by the company's lending or selling of a customer's information to outsiders who might misuse it or commit outright fraud. It is also wise for a company to retain its customers' trust.[2] It is important that a company use its customers' personal information in accordance with the law and how the use is agreed upon in its privacy policy and for no other purposes. It is also crucial that a company dispose of the information when it no longer has a need for it. Ideally, a company should establish similar relationships of trust with all of its stakeholders, both past and present. Customers tend to prefer businesses with good reputations for promoting privacy and keeping personal information secure. By holding to those principles of security and the intent of the principles in the various codes regarding the collection, use, and retention of a customer's information, a business can secure and maintain the trust of its customers and prove to its employees that they are part of a trusted institution.

Each corporate entity should carefully consider the way it complies with federal, state, provincial, and local privacy legislation and regulations that have been developed to help create consistent and universal responses to local, national, and globalized privacy agreements. One of the best ways to guarantee compliance with privacy legislation is to create appropriate privacy policies and ensure that they are followed and understood by both customers and employees. These policies should be kept updated as legislation, technologies, or social expectations change. This process can be overseen by a privacy officer or committee designated to monitor new rules imposed by government and respond to such problems as customer challenges, privacy breaches, or employees' concerns about their own privacy.

Internal and external business privacy depends on a complex matrix of legislation, regulation, policy, trust, good sense, and goodwill. One piece of pertinent legislation in the United States is the Gramm-Leach-Blilely Act, also known as the Financial Services Modernization Act, enacted in 1999 to protect all personal information held by such institutions as banks, securities firms, insurance companies, companies that lend money, tax return services, credit counselors, and real estate services. That information includes, for example, account information, social security numbers, closed-circuit TV (CCTV) images, and all personal contact information.

Another pertinent U.S. law is the Electronic Communications Privacy Act of 1986, which guarantees the security of information as it is transferred and captured (that is, during the *act* of transferring information), but not information that is *stored* on a computer system. However, there is some debate among legislators about the difference between intercepting a message during transmission and retrieving a message stored on a computer.[3]

In spite of these laws, not all of the previously cited privacy benchmarks are addressed to the same degree by all companies, according to a study carried out by the Ponemon Institute, an independent U.S. privacy and security think tank, and the Ontario Information Privacy Commissioner's (IPC) office, in Canada. In this joint study, entitled *Cross-National Study of Canadian and U.S. Corporate Privacy Practices* (2004), Ponemon and the Ontario IPC matched nineteen U.S. and nineteen Canadian companies in a survey that addressed eight areas, including privacy policy, communications and training, privacy management, data security methods, privacy compliance, choice and consent, global standards, and redress. In most categories, Canadian companies were shown to be more conscientious than their U.S. counterparts. In the study's key findings, Canadian companies appeared, on the whole, to be more likely to fulfill the requirements of the CSA's privacy code (see appendix E for examples of the study's results).

After the Ponemon/Ontario IPC's report was published, Ponemon joined other organizations, like TRUSTe, for example, to develop annual reports about and prizes for the "Most Trusted Companies in Privacy" in the United States. On its website, TRUSTe claims that it "helps thousands of businesses promote online safety and trust and guides consumers to sites that protect their online privacy."[4] TRUSTe also provides "rating seals" to alert consumers to a company's "trustworthiness." Ben Edelman[5] of the Harvard Business School, a professor and lawyer who closely follows TRUSTe and such "online trust authorities" as BBBonline (Better Business Bureau) and SiteAdvisor, has found the latter two to be more trustworthy and competent than TRUSTe. (See his website for some examples of his case studies.) As we can see, online rating efforts are still developing and require close monitoring.

DO EMPLOYEES HAVE THE RIGHT TO PRIVACY AT WORK AND, IF SO, TO WHAT DEGREE?

Not only does the privacy relationship between a company and its customers matter, the privacy relationship between an employee and an employer is also vital and depends on several scenarios determined by legal concerns or internal corporate culture. While there are privacy rights that we expect to be recognized when we are at home or in public, or in the way we deal with the government, the workplace presents a different set of issues, especially in light of the sensitivity of some kinds of information held by the employer and varying with the employee's role in a company.

Workplace privacy issues are all directly related to PI's four aspects of privacy. A company is responsible for maintaining employees' information privacy, or "data protection," unless there are mitigating circumstances, for example, a police investigation. Constitutional legislation deters employers from invading an employee's bodily privacy (for example, as it appears in the U.S. Constitution's Fourth Amendment and Sections 7 and 8 of the Canadian Charter of Rights and Freedoms).[6] However, the overwhelming use and (perceived) abuse of information and communication technologies (ICT) in the workplace has caused a great deal of and variety of surveillance of employees' use of computers, as Anton B. became aware of when his communications privacy was compromised. An employer must have reasonable grounds or suspicions of wrong doing if they plan to violate a person's territorial privacy, both in the workplace or any other public space.

Some of the typical sources of concern include whether an employer has reasonable justification for breaching employees' privacy (for example, when there is suspicion of theft) or whether an employee might benefit from selling company information to a third party. Another common concern is whether the employee and employer have negotiated a relationship based on privacy as part of a contract (that is, can an employee expect to have privacy rights at all, for example, while in the military, while working for a financial institution, while employed by a weapons manufacturer, or if a patent is at risk of being exposed or shared?).

An employee also has the responsibility of inquiring about his or her workplace privacy, for example, by seeking out corporate policies on the personal use of computers, whether it is during working hours or afterward. The optimum response to privacy concerns for an employee might be for him or her to acquire credentials and become the privacy officer for his or workplace, as outlined in the following section.

SEAL OF APPROVAL

In addition to principles regarding the collection, use, retention, and destruction of personal information created by government and companies are the responses of such corporate think tanks and professional organizations as the Conference Board of Canada and the International Association of Privacy Professionals (IAPP). In 2004, the IAPP launched its U.S. Corporate Privacy credential, the Certified Information Privacy Professional (CIPP), which in 2006 was designed to address Canadian corporate privacy issues with its CIPP/C (Canadian) designation.

EXAMPLES OF WORKPLACE PRIVACY

The employer and employee should take into account whether the potential harm done to an employee in limiting or removing his or her privacy correlates with a company's need for privacy. It is also important to determine whether, or to what degree, local, state, provincial, or federal legislation is applicable in a particular workplace. Both parties should also consider whether the employer is overstepping its legal right in the degree of privacy that it takes away from the employee.

An employee should be informed if he or she will be under surveillance by computer keystroke counting or CCTV, or subjected to biometric identification, for example, eye scans or fingerprint imprints for entrance to sensitive areas, x-ray machines, bodily intervention, drug testing, or bag checks, much as our everyman, Anton B., was faced with in chapter 2. Regarding concerns for fair workplace surveillance,[7] see the following sections (and appendix F) for examples of workplace drug and alcohol testing policies.

THE BUSINESS PERSPECTIVE: DOES THE BOSS HAVE TO RESPECT MY PRIVACY?

From the moment someone is hired and throughout the entire term of employment, surveillance by the employer is a very one-sided affair. An employee's information privacy, or "data protection," is already potentially compromised when he or she submits a résumé, which includes a phone number, an address, details of previous employment, and sometimes information that should not have been requested, for legal and ethical reasons. An employee's information privacy may also be compromised by criminal background checks. His or her bodily privacy may be eroded by invasive procedures to determine drug or alcohol use or abuse (the testing for which may be random or ongoing).

From the time of hiring, an employee's territorial privacy might be compromised in several ways. Several methods might be used to determine where an employee is, for example, by using a punch card (or biological ID methods) to show that an employee is actually in the workplace, or by deploying a GPS on a company vehicle. Privacy of communications might be compromised when the amount of work an employee is completing is questioned by means as different as keystroke counting or monitoring the "appropriate" use of company computers, as in the case of Anton B. Wise employers will create an "appropriate use" policy for ICT, and employees should seek out such policies.

COMMUNICATIONS PRIVACY

In the provocatively titled "Computer and E-mail Workplace Surveillance in Canada: The Shift from Reasonable Expectation of Privacy to Reasonable Surveillance,"[8] University of Ottawa lawyer and professor Michael Geist points to a rebalancing of the Fourth Amendment and Charter of Rights and Freedoms clauses previously cited. Cross-border influence on privacy practices is made clear when Geist says that "the Canadian perspective on computer surveillance in the workplace is significantly influenced by U.S. jurisprudence, where courts and legislators have been far more active in addressing the issue [of surveillance]."[9] By citing a number of U.S. court cases, Geist notes that employees' "reasonable expectations of privacy" will be diminished if employees use company computers for viewing pornography, communicating racist language, using stolen passwords, and disclosing information that may harm a company.[10]

BODILY PRIVACY: JUST SAY "NO" TO DRUG TESTING

One of the more contentious privacy issues in the workplace is drug and alcohol testing. In some cases, some workplace testing makes perfect sense, while in other cases such testing can seem arbitrary, without cause, fraught with hysteria, and outright reactionary. What makes sense? Drug testing is often imposed on employees working with dangerous machinery, including construction or railroad workers, or working with explosives, such as in mining or the military. It is also often required of employees who are responsible for the safety of others, bus drivers, security personnel, or life guards, for example. Employees working with highly valued commodities, like diamonds or gold, are often required to undergo some sort of bodily intrusion, for example, strip or cavity searches. But what grounds should there be to test an employee if he or she is sitting at a desk, selling simple products, or teaching history or English in classes, where there is no possibility of harm to others?

Impairment that limits any job performance should, of course, be a concern, but if someone has ingested a substance that can still be detected in the body when the employee is no longer impaired, there is disagreement about whether there are legitimate grounds for testing. (See appendix G for a debate regarding the pros and cons of drug testing in schools.) Employers' attitudes, particularly in light of the so-called war on drugs, which began in full force under President Ronald Reagan's administration, can range dramatically; however, as a way of explaining the justification for testing, John Gilliom[11] points out that the judiciary will tend to abandon an employee's privacy rights in the following circumstances:

> What [the judiciary] turn to . . . is what they depict as a balancing of the privacy concerns of workers against the state interest in conducting the search. If the privacy interests of the workers are felt to outweigh the needs of the government, then the search is unreasonable. If, on the other and more *prevalent* hand, the needs of the state outweigh the rights of the individual, then a search—even one lacking any modicum of individualized suspicion—is reasonable.[12] (emphasis added)

Ultimately, drug testing must be justified, according to lawyer Lisa Goodfellow, who published a nine-point series of questions in an article entitled "How to Implement Drug Testing."[13] She notes that drug dependency is defined as a disability in Canadian provincial and federal law and, that under human rights legislation, a person with a disability cannot be discriminated against. Her questions, designed to guide employers, are as follows:

1. Is there evidence of drug abuse in your workplace?
2. Has the requirement to drug test been forced upon your organization from an outside party?
3. Are there positions within your organization that are safety-sensitive?
4. Are these safety-sensitive positions subject to regular supervision?
5. Would your drug testing policy require preemployment tests?
6. When an employee tests positive for drug use, does the policy allow for accommodation of drug dependent employees?
7. If it is determined that an employee is substance dependent, does the policy attempt to accommodate the needs of the employee?
8. Does the drug testing policy provide for automatic termination?
9. Does the policy call for testing in any other circumstances (postaccident or other cases where it is suspected that the employee is impaired)?[14]

PRIVACY: A WORKPLACE ILLUSION

Depending on what you do for a living, expecting to live a private life at work is somewhat of an illusion, unless you are the boss and can control your own information. But respect for others' privacy might actually develop better workers. Building trust is a good way to promote better relationships, greater productivity, and a healthier atmosphere. Along with a greater trust comes respect for privacy outside of the workplace, for example, in the way we treat private information regarding healthcare, which is the topic of the next chapter.

QUESTIONS FOR DISCUSSION

1. Have you ever falsified a job application because you didn't want your prospective employer to know something about you?
2. What would you think if your employer used your personal information to his or her advantage?
3. How much personal information should an employer know about employees?
4. Have you ever been subjected to drug or alcohol testing for a job? What was the company's rationale for making you take the tests?
5. Whose rights to privacy should prevail, yours or the company's?

NOTES

1. Elin Palm, "Securing Privacy at Work: The Importance of Contextualized Consent." *Ethics of Information Technology* 11(2009): 233–41.
2. Ann Cavoukian and Tyler J. Hamilton, *The Privacy Payoff: How Successful Businesses Build Trust* (Toronto: McGraw-Hill Ryerson, 2002).
3. Cyber Telecom, "ECPA: Law Enforcement Intercepting Content: Title III." Accessed from www.cybertelecom.org/security/ecpafeds.htm.
4. TRUSTe, "About TRUSTe." Accessed from www.truste.com/about_TRUSTe/index.html
5. See www.benedelman.org.
6. The Fourth Amendment to the U.S. Constitution states, "The right of the people to be secure in their persons, houses, papers, and effects, against unreasonable searches and seizures, shall not be violated; and no Warrants shall issue but upon probable cause, supported by Oath or affirmation, and particularly describing the place to be searched, and the persons or things to be seized" (U.S. Constitution Online, "Amendment 4, Search and Seizure." Accessed from www.usconstitution.net/xconst_Am4.html). Sections 7 and 8 of

the Canadian Charter of Rights and Freedoms say the following: "7. Everyone has the right to life, liberty, and security of the person and the right not to be deprived thereof except in accordance with the principles of fundamental justice. 8. Everyone has the right to be secure against unreasonable search or seizure" (Canadian Charter of Rights and Freedoms Online, "Part 1 of the Constitution Act, 1982." Accessed from www.laws.justice.gc.ca/en/charter/).

7. See the Canadian Internet Policy and Public Interest Clinic at www .cippic.ca/workplace-privacy/#right_privacy_workplace.

8. Michael Geist, "Computer and E-mail Workplace Surveillance in Canada: The Shift from Reasonable Expectation of Privacy to Reasonable Surveillance." *Canadian Bar Review/La Revue du Barreau Canadien* 82(2) (2003): 151–89.

9. Geist, "Computer and E-mail Workplace Surveillance in Canada," 151.

10. Geist, "Computer and E-mail Workplace Surveillance in Canada," 151.

11. John Gilliom, *Surveillance, Privacy, and the Law: Employee Drug Testing and the Politics of Social Control* (Ann Arbor: University of Michigan Press, 1994).

12. Gilliom, *Surveillance, Privacy, and the Law*, 108.

13. Lisa Goodfellow, "How to Implement Drug Testing." *Focus on Canadian Employment and Equality Rights* 6(18) (June 2002): 36–48.

14. Goodfellow, "How to Implement Drug Testing," 36.

7

Privacy and Health

When I asked a Canadian biologist in a privacy focus group what she wanted to keep most private about her, she replied, "*Everything* emanating from me . . . physical, medical, and blood." Maintaining the privacy of patients' medical conditions and the records that describe them is an important contemporary concern. Health privacy includes securing information about current conditions, underlying conditions, and potential conditions suggested by family history or DNA testing. And, while recognizing that surrendering one's health information may result in more efficient service, promote research, and contribute to a universal healthcare system, this chapter illustrates some of the dangers of digitizing and transferring medical records by giving some examples of incidents that have jeopardized the security of records and, consequently, threatened patients whose sensitive medical conditions were no longer confidential.

This chapter also analyzes the conflict between a patient's rights to privacy and the necessity to disclose medical records to the right persons at the right time during times of crisis to save lives. Such situations question the sanctity of patient-doctor confidence regarding when and if a patient's health information can be disclosed without the patient's consent. These concerns are analyzed with reference to the U.S. Health Insurance Portability and Accountability Act (HIPAA) and equivalent Canadian federal legislation and provincial acts, for example, the federal Privacy Act, the Personal Information Protection and Electronic Documents Act (PIPEDA), and such provincial laws as the Ontario Personal Health Information Privacy Act (PHIPA) and other provincial freedom of information and privacy acts. When using U.S. examples, the pertinent privacy issues are referred to within the context of the U.S. model of Medicare (for seniors over age 65) and U.S. Medicaid available, not universally, but to "certain low-income individuals and families that fit into an eligibility group that is recognized by federal and state law."[1] In Canada, *Medicare* is the term used to refer to Canada's *universal* healthcare system of the same name.

There are some bewildering differences between the U.S. and Canadian health systems, especially U.S. private healthcare costs. Studies have consistently shown U.S. costs rising to the point that, in the past ten years, the Canadian healthcare system was one-third to one-half cheaper than administrative and overall care in the United States.[2] To a certain level of care, Canadians are covered universally (and therefore Canadian privacy law applies universally). In Canada, private healthcare companies cover certain medical needs not included in Medicare, for example, prescriptions and dentistry. They, too, are required to protect patients' privacy by Canadian federal and provincial laws. On the other hand, Americans' healthcare, and therefore their healthcare privacy, is protected selectively.

U.S. GOVERNMENT LAWS REGULATING HEALTH INFORMATION PRIVACY

The U.S. Department of Health and Human Services (DHHS) website[3] provides valuable information to U.S. citizens about federal "covered entities" and privacy protection and exceptions to those entities. The federal law that covers who can and cannot control (or even see) one's private information is called the Privacy Rule. The DHHS site informs us of the following:

> The Privacy Rule applies to all forms of individuals' protected health information, whether electronic, written, or oral. The Security Rule, a federal law that protects health information in electronic form, requires entities covered by HIPAA to ensure that electronic health information is secure.

The site provides information on the following:

1. who must follow the laws
2. who is not required to follow the laws
3. how information is protected

4. which rights the Privacy Rule provides individuals regarding health information
5. who can look at and receive an individual's health information

Table 7.1, downloaded from the DHHS website, provides a view of which U.S. "entities" are covered under the privacy and security rules.

The U.S. Office for Civil Rights enforces the HIPAA Privacy Rule and the HIPAA Security Rule, which set national standards for the security of electronic protected health information. The confidentiality provisions of the Patient Safety Rule protect identifiable information when it is used to analyze patient "safety events" and improve patient safety.[4] Further information on the DHHS site includes guidelines regarding the security of medical records; health information in the workplace; and which personal representatives are allowed to see the records, including family, friends, power of attorney, and executors of a will (but not someone who is determined not to have your best interest in mind).

While HIPAA (and the Privacy Rule and Security Rule) set out regulations about who can see health records and how they might be used, some U.S. private health plans are known to have broken the rules by writing to Medicare and Medicaid services recipients to tell them that they could lose their coverage because of new healthcare programs in Congress. These practices are discussed in an article published on the Center for Democracy and Technology website,[5] which

Table 7.1. Covered Entities

A Healthcare Provider	*A Health Plan*	*A Healthcare Clearinghouse*
This includes the following: • doctors • clinics • psychologists • dentists • chiropractors • nursing homes • pharmacies These providers are covered only if they transmit any information in an electronic form in connection with a transaction for which DHHS has adopted a standard.	This includes the following: • health insurance companies • HMOs • company health plans • government programs that pay for healthcare, for example, Medicare, Medicaid, and the military and veterans health care programs	This includes entities that process nonstandard health information they receive from another entity into a standard (that is, standard electronic format or data content) or vice versa.

makes it clear that using clients' personal information for anything other than a "healthcare operation" is a violation of the clients' expectations that their personal information would only be used for the purposes it was collected, that is, for healthcare operations (suggesting that the health plans' intentions were not healthcare-related, but rather political).

PROTECTING U.S. HEALTH INFORMATION: "STIMULATING PRIVACY"

In 2009, President Barack Obama implemented the American Recovery and Reinvestment Act (ARRA) in an attempt to help correct bank, real estate, and other financial meltdowns and invest in private industry (the automobile industry) and public services, most particularly healthcare. According to Dr. David Blumenthal,[6] a healthcare policy specialist and the U.S. national coordinator for health information technology,

> The law prevents dramatic state cuts in Medicaid, expands funding for preventive healthcare services and healthcare research, and helps the unemployed buy health insurance. But perhaps [ARRA's] most profound effect on doctors and patients will result from its unprecedented $19 billion program to promote the adoption and use of health information technology (HIT), especially electronic health records (EHRs).[7]

While much of Blumenthal's article is about the ideological barriers and financial incentives directed to deploying and sustaining HIT and EHRs, he makes an important observation about the privacy and security of electronic records in the hands of third parties. HITECH, as health information technology is referred to in the ARRA, now applies the privacy and security principles of HIPAA to third party companies, such as Google or Microsoft, which are helping to design and deploy programs to control EHRs. HITECH also "limits the commercial use of such information."[8] Nonetheless, a number of U.S. journalists and academics have spoken out against what they say is a potential disjuncture between cost reduction by way of EHRs and privacy guarantees. Several media releases refer to the 2011 report entitled "Privacy and Security in the Implementation of Health Information Technology (Electronic Health Records): United States and European Union Compared,"[9] which calls for better security measures in a more timely manner. Coauthor David Baumer acknowledges that savings will be realized once everyone is "connected" (only 50 percent of U.S. citizens have EHRs); however, in an interview, he stated, "We are moving in the right direction, but we have a long way to go. . . . The Obama administration's health plan relies on EHR savings as part of its effort to be revenue neutral. And more privacy protections are needed to make those savings a reality."[10]

CANADIAN GOVERNMENT LAWS REGULATING HEALTH INFORMATION PRIVACY

Canada has two federal privacy laws, the Privacy Act and PIPEDA, both of which apply to health matters in much the same way as the Privacy Rule and Security Rule in the United States. The main difference, however, is due to Canada's long-standing *universal* "Medicare" system and health privacy provisions in each province and territory. Because there is universal legislation, information that can be gathered, organized, and kept secure, on the whole, can be done so with more confidence (there have been cases of carelessness or theft) or at least with more clarity. The other difference between the two guarantees of privacy is that, in Canada, there is a federal privacy commissioner and provincial privacy commissioners, who, while working at arm's length from their respective governments, respond to privacy breaches and offer advice on how to interpret legislation, including matters related to health.

For example, the Ontario privacy commissioner's website explains the purposes of PHIPA, saying that it was established

> to protect the confidentiality of personal health information in the custody or control of health information custodians and to provide individuals with a right of access to their own personal health information and the right to seek correction of such information, with limited exceptions.

WHAT ARE THE ISSUES AND WHY SHOULD WE BE CONCERNED?

According to Maria Yin Ling Fung and John Paynter,[11] digitized health information can be at risk due to a variety of reasons, not unlike those pertaining to business and government. A lot of people can have access to electronic health records, some of whom are poorly trained or are simply careless. Chief among Fung and Paynter's concerns are the potential fragility of aging computer operating systems,[12] Trojan horse interventions, piracy, a plethora of "denials of service," and guaranteeing controlled, authoritative access. Those who may care least about keeping patient (or client) information secure are temporary employees who have nothing to gain or lose by being careful with others' privacy.

In the United States, health insurance companies, especially health maintenance organizations (HMOs), have long had the opportunity of limiting services to those who apply for insurance with "preexisting" conditions. These conditions may not even have been known to the person seeking insurance, but, in many cases, even if the condition is only discovered due to work that brings out the condition (stress, allergies, or physical labor, for example), insurance companies that demand access to health records to make their decisions about the degree of coverage might deny coverage.

THE ETHICS OF DISCLOSING PERSONAL HEALTH INFORMATION TO A THIRD PARTY

Some illnesses, such as transmissible diseases, are required by law to be disclosed for the safety of others. But other examples, such as reporting psychiatric and psychological conditions, present a gray area not always understood, often at times of great peril. Is a person's privacy jeopardized if his or her psychological condition is divulged to family, medical, or legal authorities? Legislation, policy, and common sense make it clear that divulging such information is not only possible but advisable and under some circumstances legally required, as the following events show.

One of the most horrific incidents that might have been averted by disclosing an emotional or psychological crisis occurred in 2007, at Virginia Tech, where Cho Seung-Hui murdered thirty-two students and staff. Cho was known to have had behavioral problems by a psychologist at Virginia Tech's counseling center.[13] Cho's erratic behavior was also known to students and faculty, who reported their concerns to Virginia Tech's administration. The Virginia governor's incident report[14] points out that no one was aware of what could have been done to alert and coordinate campus health officials, campus security, and police at the right time.

In the days after the massacre, media reports criticized the Virginia Tech administration for considering that Cho's privacy was more important than security. But "favoring" Cho's privacy was not to blame. Press reports did not indicate a clear understanding of privacy law as it pertains to Virginia Tech and similar situations.

For example, the Canadian newspaper the *National Post* published an August 2007 editorial entitled "Privacy Turns Deadly." The then British Columbia information and privacy commissioner, David Loukidelis, responded to the editorial by saying,

> Your editorial pinning the murderous shooting rampage at Virginia Tech on privacy is inaccurate and in itself dangerous. . . . The official report on the tragedy makes it very clear that those involved failed to properly apply privacy laws [that] did allow them to share Cho's personal information and did allow them to take action. Canadian privacy laws similarly allow disclosure and action in such cases, and privacy is not to blame for this tragedy.[15]

Three years before Loukidelis's criticism of the *National Post*, in 2004, PHIPA was made law in Ontario. The act, which immediately applied to universities, includes a section entitled "Disclosures" that states the following:

> A health information custodian may disclose personal health information about an individual if the custodian believes on reasonable grounds that the disclosure is necessary for the purpose of eliminating or reducing a significant risk of serious bodily harm to a person or group of persons.[16]

And two years before Loukidelis's reply to the editorial, his Ontario counterpart, Ann Cavoukian,[17] had already made it clear in a policy "Fact Sheet" on her website how privacy should be dealt with during times of crisis. Her "Fact Sheet" reflects the positive intentions of PHIPA. Custodians of information have a legal duty to make available usually private information under the following four circumstances:

1. public interest and grave hazards (appropriate to Virginia Tech)
2. health and safety of an individual/risk of serious harm to a person or group (appropriate to Virginia Tech)
3. disclosures to public health authorities (appropriate to Virginia Tech)
4. compassionate circumstances (reporting to parents a student's psychological condition, for example; again appropriate to Virginia Tech but also to a more recent event in Ontario)[18]

Canada's "disclosures" reflect similar advice found in two pieces of U.S. legislation, the Family Educational Rights and Privacy Act (FERPA), legislation that protects students' records, and the Clery Act, which calls for "timely warning" of crime on campus—both of which were unknown to Virginia Tech authorities or not acted upon when they needed it. In fact, in 2010, Virginia Tech was found to have broken the law by the U.S. Department of Education for not following the Clery Act during Cho's rampage.[19]

Like Ontario's PHIPA, FERPA includes conditions under which a student's records can be disclosed without the consent of the student or his or her parents or guardians. The Washington-based Family Policy Compliance Office makes clear that FERPA allows schools to disclose those records, without consent, to the following parties or under the following conditions:

1. school officials with legitimate educational interest
2. other schools to which a student is transferring
3. specified officials for audit or evaluation purposes
4. appropriate parties in connection with financial aid to a student
5. organizations conducting certain studies for or on behalf of the school
6. accrediting organizations
7. to comply with a judicial order or lawfully issued subpoena
8. appropriate officials in cases of health and safety emergencies
9. state and local authorities within a juvenile justice system, pursuant to specific state law

In both jurisdictions, disclosures for "health and safety" (PHIPA) and "health and safety emergencies" (FERPA) apply not only to mass endangerment but also to the protection of the individual in such cases as the suicide of a Carleton University student in Ottawa, in 2008, who had been in counseling for depression. An article in the *Ottawa Citizen*[20] cited Virginia Tech's revised procedures as an example of how universities should be responding to student crises, by coordinating and triaging student services in a seamless manner. The article also pointed out that the Carleton University student's parents could have been advised that she was taking antidepressants and speaking to a counselor about taking her life.

After the Virginia Tech massacre, many U.S. jurisdictions began to reevaluate and coordinate laws that already allowed administrators to alert families to their children's legal or psychological crises, although that in itself may not provide a solution, especially when parties other than the suicidal individual are involved in the death, as was the case with the Carleton University student. In April 2010, William Melchert-Dinkel,[21] a nurse from Minnesota, was charged with advising the student to commit suicide on an online chat room. He had been seeking out depressed people online and, in effect, breached the student's and others' privacy for the sake of causing their deaths.

DNA, THE DEAD, THE DISMEMBERED

There are other privacy issues relating to health that address not the whole person's psyche, as in the students' cases, but a person's physical parts, "informationalized" either when one is alive or deceased. Why should we be concerned about the privacy of our DNA, cells, genes, illnesses, or extracted or removed body parts? For example, how do health insurance companies, as previously cited, use the knowledge that a person's blood sample is known to carry the gene associated with a particular disease, such as breast cancer or Huntington's? What are the ethics of collecting, preserving, disbursing, and misusing such "information"? Whose *property* can such information be? This is an area where there is no consensus and that will continue to be negotiated by the medical profession and legislators.

QUESTIONS FOR DISCUSSION

1. Under what circumstances would you allow your or a loved one's health records to be disclosed?
2. Given "human nature," whom would you trust to handle your health records and whom would you not trust?
3. What are the benefits and weaknesses of electronic health records?
4. If you knew someone who had a transmissible disease, would you report them? Would you know to whom you should report the person?

NOTES

1. U.S. Department of Health and Human Services, "Overview of Medicaid." Accessed from www.cms.gov/MedicaidGenInfo/.

2. Center for Medical Consumers, "Health Care Administrative Costs: Canada vs. USA." October 2003. Accessed from http://findarticles.com/p/articles/mi_m0815/is_10_28/ai_108994048/.

3. U.S. Department of Health and Human Services, www.hhs.gov/ocr/privacy/hipaa/understanding/consumers/index.html.

4. U.S. Department of Health and Human Services, www.hhs.gov/ocr/privacy/.

5. Sheel Pandya, "But What about the Potential HIPAA Violation?" October 23, 2009. Accessed from www.cdt.org/blogs/sheel-pandya/what-about-potential-hipaa-violation.

6. David Blumenthal, "Stimulating the Adoption of Health Information Technology." *New England Journal of Medicine* (April 9, 2009): 1477–79.

7. Blumenthal, "Stimulating the Adoption of Health Information Technology," 1478.

8. Blumenthal, "Stimulating the Adoption of Health Information Technology," 1478.

9. David Baumer, Janine Hiller, Matthew McMullen, and Wade Chumney, "Privacy and Security in the Implementation of Health Information Technology (Electronic Health Records): United States and European Union Compared." January 2011, Boston University of Science and Technology Law.

10. Molly Merrill, "Privacy Hindering EHR Progress, Say Researchers." *Healthcare IT News*, September 21, 2010.

11. Maria Yin Ling Fung and John Paynter, "The Impact of Technology on Healthcare Privacy." In *Privacy Protection for E-Services*, George Yee, ed. (Hershey, PA: Idea Group, 2006): 56–93.

12. As long ago as 2001, U.S. observers were concerned that aging government information technology could compromise privacy. See Christopher Hoenig, "Beyond E-Government." *Government Executive* 14 (November 2001): 53.

13. Unfortunately, the Virginia Tech psychologist had left his position more than a year prior to the incident and took Cho's records with him.

14. Virginia.gov, "Report of the Virginia Tech Review Panel." April 16, 2007. Accessed from www.governor.virginia.gov/tempcontent/techpanelreport.cfm.

15. David Loukidelis, "Privacy Turns Deadly." *National Post*, August 31, 2007, p. 7.

16. PHIPA, 2004, c. 3, Sched. A, s. 40 (1).

17. Ann Cavoukian, "Fact Sheet #11: Health Information Custodians Working for Nonhealth Information Custodians." February 1, 2006. Accessed from www.ipc.on.ca/images/Resources/fact-11-e.pdf.

18. Cavoukian, "Fact Sheet #11," n.p.

19. Dena Potter, "Virginia Tech Broke Law, Failed to Warn of Shooter in 2007." *Globe and Mail*, December 10, 2010, p. 9. The Clery Act is named for Jeanne Ann Clery, a student who was raped and murdered at Lehigh University in 1986.

20. "Carleton Responds." *Ottawa Citizen*, April 22, 2008, p. A3.

21. See www.cbc.ca/news/pdf/melchert-dinkel-release.pdf for Melchert-Dinkel's story.

8

Social Networking: The Facebook Casebook

In his book *The Future of Reputation,* Daniel J. Solove[1] questions whether social networking will cause the end of privacy. This question is extremely important, given that privacy is so difficult to define, so contextual, and continually in transition. Due to the increasing "sharing" of information by social network sites (SNSs), privacy is becoming even more illusory. Such SNSs as Facebook and Google have increasingly made privacy "settings" less private, with minimal notice to users. In response, a broad range of government and public bodies, including Canadian privacy commissioners, the U.S. Federal Trade Commission (FTC), think tanks, and nongovernmental organizations (NGOs), as well as the press, have begun to pay close attention to the personal, social, and economic influences of SNSs.

In April 2010, Kurt Opsahl, senior staff attorney for the Electronic Frontier Foundation,[2] published a timeline of excerpts from Facebook's privacy policy. The timeline shows that as Facebook has grown, it appears to have changed its original purpose from bringing friends together to being a huge marketing machine. As a result, it has become more difficult for users to maintain control of their personal information. Opsahl introduced his timeline, entitled "Facebook's Eroding Privacy Policy: A Timeline,"[3] in the following way:

> Since its incorporation just over five years ago, Facebook has undergone a remarkable transformation. When it started, it was a private space for communication with a group of your choice. Soon, it transformed into a platform where much of your information is public by default. Today, it has become a platform where you have no choice but

> to make certain information public, and this public information may be shared by Facebook with its partner websites and used to target ads. To help illustrate Facebook's shift away from privacy, we have highlighted some excerpts from Facebook's privacy policies over the years. Watch closely as your privacy disappears, one small change at a time.[4]

Opsahl's opening example, from 2005, shows that Facebook would not allow *any* of a user's information to be shown to *anyone* other than someone in "at least one of the groups specified by you in your privacy settings."[5] That ironclad guarantee began to crumble only the next year. After acknowledging that users perhaps wouldn't want everyone to see their information, the following rhetorical shift in the policy appeared: "Our default privacy settings limit the information displayed in your profile to your school, your specified local area, and *other reasonable community limitations that we will tell you about*" (emphasis added).[6] As with other policies, regulations, and legislation, the appearance of the word "reasonable" should raise suspicions. Who decides what is reasonable for whom? And by what means would Facebook tell users about the *other reasonable community limitations*?

By 2007, users were told that "your name, school name, and profile picture thumbnail will be available in search results across the Facebook network *unless you alter your privacy settings*" (emphasis added).[7] This policy, in effect, indemnified Facebook by placing an increased onus on users to read and be familiar with the website's privacy policy. An article in the *New York Times*[8] observes that Facebook's complex policy is longer than the U.S. Constitution. The article is critical of the way Facebook's "privacy policy" allows personal information to be shared by third parties—parties unknown to the Facebook member—unless he or she opts out by changing his or her increasingly complex settings. And while daunting, reading such policies is advisable (to see, at the least, whether the organization holds to its own privacy policy); however, it is rare that many users do so, according to a number of surveys and other studies.[9] If users read privacy policies, there is a good chance that they do not understand them, as pointed out in chapter 4. Opsahl quotes part of the privacy policy from 2009, which stated the following:

> Certain categories of information, such as your name, profile photo, list of friends, pages you are a fan of, gender, geographic region, and networks you belong to, *are considered publicly available to everyone*, including Facebook-enhanced applications, and therefore do not have privacy settings. You can, however, limit the ability of others to find this information through search using your search privacy settings.[10] (emphasis added)

In another analysis, Opsahl discusses Facebook's "Connections," a feature that makes almost all users' personal information available to many more people, even if they don't want it to be seen.[11] What is worse is that, at the time of this writing, users cannot opt out of this feature. Opsahl points out six particularly alarming aspects of "Connections." First, and most significantly, "Facebook will not let you share any . . . [personal] information without using Connections."[12] This has many adverse implications for users. As Opsahl notes, "Facebook will not respect your old privacy settings in this transition . . . if you previously sought to share your interests with 'only Friends.' Facebook will now . . . share your Connections with 'Everyone.'"[13] Thus, information that was previously revealed selectively has become available to "everyone" by default.

Another example of Facebook's increasing control over personal information is clear in Opsahl's next observation that "Facebook has removed your ability to restrict its use of this [personal] information."[14] To demonstrate Facebook's increasing control over users' information, Opsahl quotes Facebook's privacy policy, saying,

> Such information may, for example, be accessed by everyone on the Internet (including people not logged into Facebook), be indexed by third-party search engines, and be imported, exported, distributed, and redistributed by us and others without privacy limitations.[15]

Not only is Facebook distributing user information "without privacy limitations," "Facebook will continue to store and use your Connections even after you delete them. . . . We've . . . received reports that Facebook continues to use deleted profile information to help people find you through Facebook's search engine."[16] As a result, efforts to escape Facebook, or to hide activities that you no longer want to be public, or to protect yourself from unwanted attention, are becoming almost impossible.

Facebook's "Connections" has even more ways of tracking your information and linking it to other users unbeknownst to you. "Facebook sometimes creates a Connection when you 'Like' something. . . . It too can sometimes add a Connection to your profile, without you even knowing it," writes Opsahl.[17] Facebook may also create a "Connection" when you post to your wall. Opsahl provides an example of what might happen when he notes that if you use a word like FBI, "then it may show up on the Connections page, without you even knowing it."[18] Together, these elements of Facebook's "Connections" take control of user information and make it available to a wide number of unknown users for Facebook's commercial gain.

In May 2010, citing many of the same issues addressed by Opsahl, the U.S.-based Electronic Privacy Information Center (EPIC)[19] filed a thirty-eight-page "Complaint, Request for Investigation, Injunction, and Other Relief"[20] with the FTC against Facebook. EPIC represents fourteen other influential NGOs and not-for-profit research bodies, or "Petitioners," the names and URLs of which are provided in appendix H. The "Complaint" includes descriptions of each of the Petitioners' roles in defending privacy and consumers' interests. The "Complaint" is especially valuable for describing Facebook's transgressions in great detail. Section B of the "Complaint," significantly entitled "Facebook Has Made User Information 'Publicly Available' *in Violation of its Privacy Policy*" (emphasis added), points to twenty errors committed by Facebook. In Section B II, *"Facebook's Privacy Policy Is Misleading and Inconsistent with the Site's Representations"* (typeface as in the "Complaint"), the Petitioners introduce examples of "Unfair and Deceptive Practices, subject to review by the Federal Trade Commission (the 'Commission') under Section 5 of the Federal Trade Commission Act."[21]

GOOGLE

Google brought out its own form of social networking in February 2010, when it introduced a new service called "Buzz" as part of its "Gmail" (Google Mail) package in an effort to get into the social networking market by creating a way to keep contacts as close (and as *available* to other users and corporations) as those on Facebook. But, instead of calling the contacts "connections," on Buzz they are "followers," a concept that brings to mind religious or dictatorial zeal. This new application is contrary to many of the privacy models and standards referred to throughout this book.

In its original form, Buzz allowed anyone to see a list of a user's most often e-mailed contacts by automatically "opting-in" all of its users without asking them if they had any objection. That disclosure of personal information—possibly exposing unknown or disapproved of relationships—got the attention of users, nonusers, and many international data protection watchdogs. The privacy commissioner of Canada, Jennifer Stoddart, and her counterparts from France, Germany, Israel, Ireland, the Netherlands, New Zealand, Spain, and the United Kingdom, sent a letter[22] to Eric Schmidt, chairman and CEO of Google. The letter, published in Toronto's *Globe and Mail*, refers to previous Google privacy shortcomings and concludes with a list of principles similar to the Canadian Standards Association's *Model Code for the Protection of Personal Information*, the Federal Trade Commission's Fair Information Practice Principles, and the Organisation for Economic Co-operation and Development's *Guidelines on the Protection of Privacy and Transborder Flows of Personal Data*. It reads as follows:

> We . . . call on you, like all organizations entrusted with people's personal information, to incorporate fundamental privacy principles directly into the design of new online services. That means, at a minimum:
>
> - collecting and processing only the minimum amount of personal information necessary to achieve the identified purpose of the product or service;
> - providing clear and unambiguous information about how personal information will be used to allow users to provide informed consent;
> - creating privacy-protective default settings;
> - ensuring that privacy control settings are prominent and easy to use;
> - ensuring that all personal data is adequately protected; and
> - giving people simple procedures for deleting their accounts and honoring their requests in a timely way.[23]

In an article entitled "Privacy Police Take Aim at Social Media Giants,"[24] which appeared in the *Globe and Mail* the same day, Privacy Commissioner Stoddart was quoted as saying that although she and her international counterparts were concerned about all websites and Internet companies, they "focused on Google as a proxy for those firms, singling out the world's most popular search engine."[25]

EPIC had already sent its concerns about Google to the FTC two months earlier, pointing out that, in its first incarnation, Buzz violated *consumer protection law*, a certain way to get the government's attention. By the time the privacy commissioners had sent their concerns to Google, it had already changed the service so that it would "merely suggest contacts for its users' social networks,"[26] and not require them to "opt-out" to keep their e-mail contacts private.

Nonetheless, a class-action privacy suit was brought against Google that took several months to resolve and cost the company $8.5 million.[27] Interestingly, while both Facebook and Google have had constant run-ins with government, privacy watchdogs, and users, their privacy problems, in part, derive from their original, different purposes. In "Facebook and Google: Contrasts in Privacy," Tony Bradley[28] points out that

> Google is the monolithic Big Brother of the Internet, crawling and indexing every last byte of data that exists and presenting it to the general public in a matter of milliseconds through it various search offerings.[29]

And in a relatively lighthearted response to Google's clumsy, more recent attempt to capture and share its Gmail members' information (not unlike Facebook, as previously pointed out), Molly Wood[30] "rants" (her own word),

> I love the idea of neat new tech innovations that lead to streamlined communication . . . I do not, however, like a product that bursts through my door like a tornado and opts me in to a wanton in-box clutter . . . and publicly reveals my personal contact list without asking me. . . . That, right there, is bad behavior, and given all the hue and cry about Facebook's inexorable attempts to expose everything about its users to the entire world, Google ought to know better.[31]

Given these observations and the almost daily revelations about Facebook and Google overstepping our privacy expectations, it can only be said that we have to keep our eyes open for further transgressions, for example, Google's "Street View."

GOOGLE'S OTHER PROBLEMS

Before the controversy surrounding Buzz, Google already had other, perhaps more grave privacy problems that it has been gradually addressing. Google "Street View," related to Google Maps, was introduced in 2007 and "was not universally well-received."[32] The service lets viewers see streetscapes at a 360-degree angle, as photographed from the roof of a moving vehicle. To achieve the 360-degree view, the software in the "Street View" cameras is tagged with GPS data.

Initially, Google saw few problems in uploading and archiving candid street scenes that included people's faces; scantily clad young women sunbathing; and a famous shot of a man climbing over a locked gate, the image of which became known as "Break-in in progress."[33] Google invaded privacy in other ways when staff drove on well-marked private roads, past no trespassing signs, without regard for owners' wishes to "be let alone," which led to at least one lawsuit.

In "Google Street View Continues to Raise Privacy Concerns,"[34] Brian Cooper describes a couple's effort to sue Google after photographers drove up the couple's lane and took close-up shots of their house. When the couple complained, Google removed the photos from its site but responded, "Complete privacy does not exist in this world except in a desert, and anyone who is not a hermit must expect and endure the ordinary incidents of the community life of which he (or she) is a part."[35] But if a stranger is driving up your private road snapping photographs, is that one of the "*ordinary* incidents of the community life"? Incidents like this point to how vulnerable our territorial and informational privacy can be if we are not vigilant.

Three years later, in 2010, it appeared that Google had not yet learned its lesson, when it was revealed that since 2007 the company had been collecting lots of personal unencrypted WiFi data, known as "payload data," when it outfitted its Google "Street View" cars with the software code to do so. The issue became public when German privacy authorities requested that Google conduct an information audit. Google's immediate response from the company's cofounder, Sergey Brin, was, "We screwed up. I'm not going to make any excuses about this."[36] But that apology did nothing to assuage the anger of international privacy watchdogs. Among other revelations, it was discovered that Google collected information from some U.S. politicians who had unencrypted WiFi and whose houses appear on "Street View." The extent of public dismay was reflected in the press when dozens of articles appeared in May 2010, after Google acknowledged its "screw up."

Politicians, consumer watchdogs, and European privacy authorities called for an investigation into what Google had been doing with the "payload data" as consumer information. The FTC's Fair Information Practice Principles once again make it clear that if breaching privacy is a business (or "payload") issue, it is taken very seriously. In a *Washington Post* article[37] about Google's revelation of mishandling information, online security expert Hemu Nigam uses Facebook's controversies as examples of the negative effects of not taking privacy seriously when she says the following:

> Companies need to think of privacy holistically and up front so problems don't happen like they did for Facebook. . . . A venture capitalist that doesn't see privacy and security in a business plan should reject it or make sure that gets in. Because in the end it's all about good branding, and when you lose that, your advertisers bail out and so do customers.[38]

But it is difficult for citizens to "bail out" of an enterprise as powerful as Google, which has already accumulated immense amounts of personal information for commercial use from Web searches and "Street View." Nigam's concern is venture capitalists, but those of us who rely on "social capital," that is, the quantity and quality of our daily social interactions, should be intensely concerned about our personal privacy. We must be vigilant if we are going to keep our personal information safe, keep our identities safe, and protect our friendships with true friends. As long as other people are making decisions about our privacy—whatever privacy has become—we cannot achieve, or even know, what perfect privacy is. As long as there is money to be made, Google and Facebook certainly won't protect our privacy, or clearly explain what privacy is.

QUESTIONS FOR DISCUSSION

1. Do you read *every* privacy policy provided by such services as Facebook *completely*?
2. If you found a discrepancy (or outright falsehood) in an ICT service policy, would you complain to the company or find another place to report the problem?
3. What would be the best place to report the problem?
4. For what reasons do you use Facebook, Google services, or any other social networking sites?
5. Do you care about your privacy settings?

NOTES

1. Daniel J. Solove, *The Future of Reputation: Gossip, Rumor, and Privacy on the Internet* (New Haven, CT: Yale University Press, 2007).
2. Electronic Frontier Foundation, www.eff.org/about.
3. Kurt Opsahl, "Facebook's Eroding Privacy Policy: A Timeline." April 28, 2010. Accessed from www.eff.org/deeplinks/2010/04/facebook-timeline.
4. Opsahl, "Facebook's Eroding Privacy Policy," n.p.
5. Opsahl, "Facebook's Eroding Privacy Policy," n.p.
6. Opsahl, "Facebook's Eroding Privacy Policy," n.p.
7. Opsahl, "Facebook's Eroding Privacy Policy," n.p.
8. Nick Bilto, "Price of Facebook Privacy?: Start Clicking." *New York Times*, May 12, 2010. Accessed from www.nytimes.com/2010/05/13/technology/personaltech/13basics.html.

9. Susan E. Gindin, "Nobody Reads Your Privacy Notice?: It's Time for a New One!" Accessed from www.info-law.com/nobodyreads.html.
10. Opsahl, "Facebook's Eroding Privacy Policy," n.p.
11. Kurt Opsahl, "Six Things You Need to Know about Facebook Connections." May 4, 2010. Accessed from www.eff.org/deeplinks/2010/05/things-you-need-know-about-facebook.
12. Opsahl, "Six Things You Need to Know about Facebook Connections," n.p.
13. Opsahl, "Six Things You Need to Know about Facebook Connections," n.p.
14. Opsahl, "Six Things You Need to Know about Facebook Connections," n.p.
15. Opsahl, "Six Things You Need to Know about Facebook Connections," n.p.
16. Opsahl, "Six Things You Need to Know about Facebook Connections," n.p.
17. Opsahl, "Six Things You Need to Know about Facebook Connections," n.p.
18. Opsahl, "Six Things You Need to Know about Facebook Connections," n.p.
19. Electronic Privacy Information Center, http://epic.org/epic/about.html.
20. Electronic Privacy Information Center, "Before the Federal Trade Commission, Washington DC: Complaint, Request for Investigation, Injunction, and Other Relief." May 5, 2010. Accessed from http://epic.org/privacy/facebook/EPIC_FTC_FB_Complaint.pdf.
21. Electronic Privacy Information Center, "Before the Federal Trade Commission," 1.
22. Jennifer Stoddart et al., "Text of Letter to Google." *Globe and Mail*, April 20, 2010. Accessed from www.theglobeandmail.com/news/technology/text-of-letter-to-google/article1540327/.
23. Stoddart et al., "Text of Letter to Google," n.p.
24. Jacquie McNish and El Akkad, "Privacy Police Take Aim at Social Media Giants." *Globe and Mail*, April 20, 2010. Accessed from www.theglobeandmail.com/news/technology/privacy-police-take-aim-at-social-media-giants/article1541097/.
25. McNish and Akkad, "Privacy Police Take Aim at Social Media Giants," n.p.
26. Joelle Tessler, "Privacy Group Files FTC Complaint over Google Buzz." *Huffington Post*, February 17, 2010. Accessed from www.huffingtonpost.com/2010/02/17/google-buzz-privacy-conce_0_n_465215.html.
27. Robert McMillan. "Google Settles Buzz Privacy Lawsuit." *Computer World*, September 3, 2010. Accessed from www.computerworld.com/s/article/9183638/Google_settles_Buzz_privacy_lawsuit.
28. Tony Bradley, "Facebook and Google: Contrasts in Privacy." *PC World*, December 12, 2009. Accessed from www.pcworld.com/businesscenter/article/184537/facebook_and_google_contrasts_in_privacy.html.

29. Bradley, "Facebook and Google," n.p.

30. Molly Wood, "Google Buzz: Privacy Nightmare." *CNet News*, February 1, 2010. Accessed from http://news.cnet.com/8301-31322_3-10451428-256.html.

31. Wood, "Google Buzz," n.p.

32. Randall Stross, *Planet Google: One Company's Audacious Plan to Organize Everything We Know* (New York: Free Press, 2008), 144–45.

33. Stross, *Planet Google*, 145.

34. Brian Cooper, "Google Street View Continues to Raise Privacy Concerns." February 2, 2009. Accessed from www.searchengineguide.com/brian-cooper/google-street-view-continues-to-raise-pr.php.

35. Cited in Cooper, "Google Street View Continues to Raise Privacy Concerns," n.p.

36. Damon Poeter, "Google Faces Backlash over Street View, Privacy Issues." May 19, 2010. Accessed from www.crn.com/news/applications-os/224900445/google-faces-backlash-over-street-view-privacy-issues.htm.

37. Cited in Cecilia Kang, "Growing Anger over Google Street View Privacy Breach." *Washington Post*, May 10, 2010. Accessed from http://voices.washingtonpost.com/posttech/2010/05/the_anger_is_growing_over.html.

38. Cited in Kang, "Growing Anger over Google Street View Privacy Breach," n.p.

9

Conclusion: Does Privacy Have a Future?

Throughout this book I ask questions about a variety of "privacies" by relying on Privacy International's four privacy characteristics, by evaluating privacy policy and legislation, and by taking into account my genuine interest in understanding how and why people are or are not attentive to their privacy. In chapter 1, "Privacy: From Space to Cyberspace," I point out that while privacy has always been observed as a social concept by ancient, early modern, modern, and contemporary thinkers, much of humankind's views on the subject were forever changed when electronic information and communication technologies (ICTs) began to provide the means for a kind of "totalitarian technocracy"[1] by which we have allowed ourselves to be ruled. Many of us, or enough of us, took part in the social construction (or destruction) of our privacy by adopting the technology—and the attitude—that created the "information economy" at the cost of secure privacy in a more humane "information society."

Chapter 2, "A Contrast between Pre-ICT Privacy and Today's ICT Realities," provides a look at privacy before electricity changed the way we kept ourselves, our information, and our property secure. Chapter 2 also provides an intense look at a typical day for a typical person in our contemporary "panopticon" world. *Privacy: A Manifesto* paints a clear picture about how our every public move makes our privacy vulnerable.

In chapter 3, "Did ICT Create a New Social Norm?," I define and expand upon early ICT phenomena by introducing the way legal experts in the nineteenth century, namely U.S. Supreme Court justices

Samuel D. Warren and Louis D. Brandeis, concluded that our privacy should allow us to "be let alone," if we wish to be. Chapter 3 also introduces such contemporary technology gurus as Mark Zuckerberg, whose Facebook has challenged privacy by allowing too much information to fall too easily into too many hands.

In the following chapter, "Privacy Legislation and Policy: Illusory Protection?," I introduce recent and current standards developed in response to ICT and the transfer of information for personal and business reasons. Chapter 5, "Surveillance: Privacy Denied," looks at the illusion of privacy in the post-9/11 world and how we must endure increasingly intrusive measures that supposedly guarantee our safety.

In chapter 6, "Privacy in the Workplace," I provide examples of why Anton B.'s less-than-private day on the job is not, by any means, an exaggeration. The next chapter, "Privacy and Health," tells a cautionary tale about under which circumstances personal information should be shared to save lives. The final chapter concentrates on social networking sites and companies that gather, organize, and disclose our personal information, without our knowledge or permission.

WHAT, THEN, ABOUT THE FUTURE OF PRIVACY?

One thing that is certain about the future of privacy is that as we develop the capacity to gather and organize more information, the more information will be disclosed, either accidentally or intentionally, for someone else's benefit, particularly such third parties as corporate entities eager to create our marketing profile. As Randall Stross notes in *Planet Google: One Company's Audacious Plan to Organize Everything We Know*,[2]

> Putting our most personal information on the same servers that hold publicly accessible information triggers anxieties that Google's reassurances about privacy protections can never completely quell. . . . We are only too happy to avail ourselves of greatly improved access to information about others, but then, oblivious to our inconsistency, we object to others having greater access to information about ourselves.[3]

It appears, then, that information and communication technologies have a hand in transforming the norm of privacy itself, as Mark Zuckerberg suggested in 2010, and have eclipsed our ability to be private, or to *withdraw*, as Aristotle put it. But what can we do about it today? In some respects, we are all like Anton B. in that we live in the "surveillance society," under the gaze of the electronic panopticon; however, there are ways we can limit what is known about us.

First, if you must work online, be cautious of who acquires your personal information, what they do with it, how long they keep it, and what they do with it when they are finished with it. Be responsible with your and other people's information technology by keeping your passwords safe and encrypting what you can. Join the growing number of people who are withdrawing from Facebook[4] and other social network sites by committing a kind of "Facebook suicide,"[5] or just don't join in the first place. Make yourself invisible to the online spammers and hackers. Keep your information to yourself, if you can.

NOTES

1. Neil Postman, *Technopoly: The Surrender of Culture to Technology* (New York: Vintage Books, 1993), 48.
2. Randall Stross, *Planet Google: One Company's Audacious Plan to Organize Everything We Know* (New York: Free Press, 2008).
3. Stross, *Planet Google*, 151.
4. As almost 33,000 Facebook members did on "Quit Facebook Day," on June 1, 2010. See "Facebook Group Quits Social Networking Site in Protests." *Ottawa Citizen*, June 1, 2010. Accessed from ww.ottawacitizen.com/technology/tech-biz/Facebook+group+quits+social+site+protest/3097623/story.html?=3097623.
5. Micah M. White, "Facebook Suicide: The More Facebook Infringes upon People's Privacy, the More People Need to Kill Their Connection with the Social Networking Site." June 2008. Accessed from www.adbusters.org/magazine/77/facebook_suicide.html. The so-called Web 2.0 Suicide Machine app was launched in December 2009 to escape from Facebook, Twitter, LinkedIn, and MySpace. The app was met with stiff resistance from Facebook, who cut off access from Suicide Machine servers not long after the service was announced.

Appendix A

Canadian Standards Association Principles in Summary[1]

Ten interrelated principles form the basis of the Canadian Standards Association's (CSA) *Model Code for the Protection of Personal Information*. Each principle must be read in conjunction with the accompanying commentary: "CSA's . . . Code . . . sets out ten principles that balance the privacy rights of individuals and the information requirements of private organizations. . . . [T]he CSA has published a suite of companion resources to help organizations put the Code into practice, wherever you do business in the world today."[2]

1. Accountability
An organization is responsible for personal information under its control and shall designate an individual or individuals who are accountable for the organization's compliance with the following principles.

2. Identifying Purposes
The purposes for which personal information is collected shall be identified by the organization at or before the time the information is collected.

3. Consent
The knowledge and consent of the individual are required for the collection, use, or disclosure of personal information, except where inappropriate.

4. Limiting Collection
The collection of personal information shall be limited to that which is necessary for the purposes identified by the organization. Information shall be collected by fair and lawful means.

5. Limiting Use, Disclosure, and Retention
Personal information shall not be used or disclosed for purposes other than those for which it was collected, except with the consent of the individual or as required by law. Personal information shall be retained only as long as necessary for the fulfillment of those purposes.

6. Accuracy
Personal information shall be as accurate, complete, and up-to-date as is necessary for the purposes for which it is to be used.

7. Safeguards
Personal information shall be protected by security safeguards appropriate to the sensitivity of the information.

8. Openness
An organization shall make readily available to individuals specific information about its policies and practices relating to the management of personal information.

9. Individual Access
Upon request, an individual shall be informed of the existence, use, and disclosure of his or her personal information and shall be given access to that information. An individual shall be able to challenge the accuracy and completeness of the information and have it amended as appropriate.

10. Challenging Compliance
An individual shall be able to address a challenge concerning compliance with the above principles to the designated individual or individuals accountable for the organization's compliance.

NOTES

1. Reprinted with permission of the Canadian Standards Association.
2. CSA Principles in Summary, www.csa.ca/cm/ca/en/privacy-code/publications/view-privacy-code.

Appendix B

Freedom of Information and Protection of Privacy at Wilfrid Laurier University, Office of the Privacy Coordinator[1]

Wilfrid Laurier University operates within the ambit of Ontario's Freedom of Information and Protection of Privacy Act (FIPPA).[2] We also have institutional guidelines concerning these matters. In most cases, the guidelines offer simple, direct, and inexpensive access to personal information. These guidelines are recorded as policies "10.1 Information Availability and Privacy Protection" and "10.2 Student Records." In some cases, where the institutional policies of the University are irrelevant or silent, FIPPA may be of use. In situations where the University's institutional guidelines and the FIPPA conflict, the Act prevails. Relevant items of interest may be found in the area to the left. Students, applicants, and others who give personal information to the University should read our "Notice of Collection." Employees and others using information collected by the University should read our FIPPA "Compliant Practices." This can be accessed by clicking on the item on website cited below.

NOTES

1. See www.wlu.ca/homepage.php?grp_id=1779 for further details about Wilfrid Laurier University's privacy model.
2. See Ontario's Freedom of Information and Personal Privacy Act at www.e-laws.gov.on.ca/html/statutes/english/elaws_statutes_90f31_e.htm.

Appendix C

Wilfrid Laurier University: Notice of Collection and Examples of Use or Disclosure

NOTICE OF COLLECTION

Wilfrid Laurier University collects personal information under the authority of the Wilfrid Laurier University Act. Personal information collected by any part of the University may be used or disclosed by other units in order to execute the various functions of the University and to administer the various relations between the University and its students, alumni, employees, clients, suppliers, partners, and others. If you have questions about this collection, please contact the director of Laurier's University Information and Privacy Office.

EXAMPLES OF USE OR DISCLOSURE

Laurier uses and discloses personal information in ways that are directly implied by the above notice and also ways that are consistent with the above notice. The following are some examples of the uses and disclosures that relate to the execution and administration of the various relations and functions of the University.

Personal information is used to create and maintain a public record of Laurier's graduates. The names of, and degrees received by, graduates of the University are a matter of public record. Normally, educational history other than this is not public and can be released only by the student through requests for the distribution, by the University, of official transcripts or official letters.

The names, programs, and other similar personal information of the recipients of honours, such as inclusion on a dean's list or receipt of a scholarship, are used by the University to create and maintain a public record. This information is published in a number of forms. Many scholarships, bursaries, and prizes have specific additional collection and disclosure conditions. Laurier assumes that persons applying for scholarships, bursaries, and prizes have agreed to the relevant conditions.

Unless directed otherwise by a student, Laurier may disclose contact information of graduating students to organizations providing convocation-related services, such as photography and degree-framing.

Voluntary membership on teams representing Laurier or participation in events as a representative of Laurier is considered an agreement by the member or participant to the public disclosure of limited personal information, such as name, degree program, and other team or event-related information.

Names of students are collected by the University in order to operate both virtual and physical classroom environments. By registering in courses, students recognize and agree that their names may be divulged, both orally and in written form, to other members of the student body during activities such as, but not limited to, taking attendance, assigning topics, organizing students for group work, assessing classroom participation, facilitating classroom discussion, and organizing tutorials. Students who are concerned about such disclosures should contact the course instructor to identify whether there are any possible alternatives to such disclosure.

Some courses must, due to the material involved and the approach to evaluation embraced by the instructor, utilize services that help detect plagiarism. The use of these services is meant to ensure the realization of educational outcomes in courses and to promote the integrity of the credentials granted by the University. Materials submitted in courses may also be retained by the University for use and disclosure as exemplars, in course design and evaluation. By registering in these courses, students acknowledge and accept that some of their personal information may need to be submitted to these services, and that their submissions may be retained for future use.

In order to allow for their elections and other core operations, the University may provide personal information of students to the Wilfrid Laurier University Students' Union, Graduate Student Association, and other similar organizations. The University may also use personal information of students to collect fees on behalf of the Wilfrid Laurier University Students' Union and other student organizations. By agreement with student organizations, the University, on behalf of these organizations, discloses students' personal information to insurers selected by the students' associations.

Personal information is used or disclosed to determine eligibility for scholarships, bursaries, and other forms of student aid and to promote the availability of such assistance.

Address, telephone, e-mail, and other information may be used to contact you, by any unit within the University, including our ancillary services and external agencies involved in the collection of fees and fines owing to the University. This includes the collection of fines for parking-related infractions.

Personal information may by transferred to ministries and agencies of the Ontario Government and the Government of Canada as required by statute or regulation. This includes transfers to entities such as Statistics Canada and the Ministry of Training Colleges and Universities.

Registration records, educational history, and supporting documents, including records of misconduct, may be used for the adjudication of admission, progression, and graduation with respect to various programs. Such information may be transmitted to other educational institutions and partners involved in the delivery of programs offered at, with, or through Laurier, including, but not limited to, entities involved in the provision of joint degrees, cross-registration, practicums, exchanges, placements, co-op positions, and service-learning opportunities.

Personal information is used by the University to create various statistical and analytical reports that guide in planning and administration. It may also be transferred to external entities involved in research and statistical analysis of student experience and accomplishment, in order to improve the quality and effectiveness of the University's programs, policies, and practices. E-mail addresses of samples of the student body may be provided to organizations that collect student opinions regarding various aspects of the quality of the educational environment provided by the University. Examples of such research and analyses include the National Survey of Student Engagement, administered from Indiana University, USA, and the Public Economics Data Analysis Laboratory project directed from McMaster University, Canada.

Personal information is used to create class lists, grade submission lists, and other materials needed by employees of the University. This includes the utilization of pictures of students collected and intended primarily for inclusion on Laurier's One Card.

Personal information may be collected, used, and disclosed in disciplinary or security procedures.

Personal information may be used for institutional development and fundraising programs and initiatives. This includes disclosures of personal information to the alumni association and to independent commercial ventures that become partners of the University or the association in fundraising activities. All persons registered at Laurier are considered members of our alumni. Alumni may instruct the alumni association to refrain from using their personal information for development purposes.

Applicants may be contacted about admission opportunities other than those specifically identified by the applicant. They may also be contacted to guide the improvement of the University's services and offerings.

Appendix D

The Difference between Security and Privacy

Since the events of 9/11, when the twin towers were destroyed by terrorists in New York City, airline and other security has changed dramatically. As the following text indicates, airline passengers are now subject to the U.S. Department of Homeland Security's Transportation Security Administration (TSA) baggage inspection. Their "Notice of Baggage Inspection" is now found by some passengers in their luggage once they arrive at their destinations. In addition to the notice, TSA's website provides important advice about safe traveling and the measures a traveler should take for a hassle-free flight.[1] The following is a reprint of the notice.

NOTICE OF BAGGAGE INSPECTION[2]

To protect you and your fellow passengers, the Transportation Security Administration (TSA) is required by law* to inspect all baggage. As part of this process, some bags are opened and physically inspected. Your bag was among those selected for physical inspection.

During the inspection, your bag and its contents may have been searched for prohibited items. At the completion of the inspection, the contents were returned to your bag.

If the TSA security officer was unable to open your bag because it was locked, the officer may have been forced to break the locks on your bag. TSA sincerely regrets having to do this, however, TSA is not liable for damage to your locks resulting from this necessary security precaution.

For packing tips and suggestions on how to secure your baggage during your next trip, please visit www.tsa.gov.

We appreciate your understanding and cooperation. If you have questions, comments, or concerns, please feel free to contact the TSA Contact Center:

Phone: 866.289.9673 (toll free)
e-mail: TSA-ContactCenter@dhs.gov

*Section 110(b) of the Aviation and Transportation Security Act of 2001, 49 U.S.C. 44901(c)-(e)

Rev. 6.1.2004 Smart Security Saves Time

NOTES

1. Transportation Security Administration, www.tsa.gov.
2. Reprinted by permission of the TSA.

Appendix E

Ponemon Institute / Information Privacy Commissioner of Ontario Corporate Privacy Comparisons

Examples of the outcome of a joint study entitled *Cross-National Study of Canadian and U.S. Corporate Privacy Practices* (2004), conducted by the Ponemon Institute and the Ontario Information Privacy Commissioner, matched nineteen U.S. and nineteen Canadian companies.

COMPARISONS

1. Canadian companies are more likely to have a "dedicated privacy officer or leader responsible for privacy issues than comparable U.S. companies . . . a clearly articulated strategy, mission, and charter . . . privacy leaders are more likely to have high level reporting authority and access to significant resources within their organization."
2. Canadian companies are more likely to have a "formal redress process for customers and other stakeholders to respond to queries and concerns about how personal information is used, shared, and retained. . . . Canadian companies are more open to providing customers with access rights to see and correct personal information collected about them."
3. Canadian policies "appear to offer more choices to customers and consumers in terms of opting out (or opting in) to secondary uses and sharing . . . while data sharing with third parties is a common practice in both Canada and the United States,

none of the Canadian companies actually permitted the sale of customer data."

4. Canadian companies are more likely to offer privacy training or awareness programs for employees and contractors who handle sensitive personal information.
5. Corporate marketers in Canadian companies appear to be more involved in their company's privacy initiatives.
6. Canadian companies "appear to hold their vendors and other third parties to higher standards or due diligence requirements. . . . There is no clear evidence, however, that Canadian companies are more aggressive at monitoring or enforcing these standards."
7. Canadian companies appear to have a more aggressive data control orientation when collecting and retaining sensitive personal information. Canadian companies are more concerned about insider misuse than external penetration.
8. Canadian companies "appear to require more rigorous data quality controls . . . especially when the application involves transborder movement."
9. U.S. companies "use more rigorous data security mechanisms and controls to prevent potential hackers from penetrating the company's IT core and data warehouses."
10. U.S. companies "are less likely to have strict policies that protect the privacy of employees' personal data. . . . In Canadian companies there are few policies governing the monitoring and surveillance of employee computer usage in the workplace."
11. Both Canadian and U.S. companies have a difficult time measuring the effectiveness of specific controls intended to reduce privacy risks.
12. Both Canadian and U.S. companies have an equally difficult time proving the economic value of privacy and data on corporate profitability (return of investment, or ROI).

Appendix F

Drug-Free Workplace Policy

The Texas Workforce Commission's "Drug-Free Workplace Policy"[1] provides a template for designing similar policies in a variety of circumstances. The following is a reprint of the policy.[2]

DRUG-FREE WORKPLACE POLICY

It is the purpose of XYZ Corporation, Inc., (the Company) to help provide a safe and drug-free work environment for our clients and our employees. With this goal in mind and because of the serious drug abuse problem in today's workplace, we are establishing the following policy for existing and future employees of XYZ Corporation, Inc.

The Company explicitly prohibits:

- The use, possession, solicitation for, or sale of narcotics or other illegal drugs, alcohol, or prescription medication without a prescription on Company or customer premises or while performing an assignment.
- Being impaired or under the influence of legal or illegal drugs or alcohol away from the Company or customer premises, if such impairment or influence adversely affects the employee's work performance, the safety of the employee or of others, or puts at risk the Company's reputation.

- Possession, use, solicitation for, or sale of legal or illegal drugs or alcohol away from the Company or customer premises, if such activity or involvement adversely affects the employee's work performance, the safety of the employee or of others, or puts at risk the Company's reputation.
- The presence of any detectable amount of prohibited substances in the employee's system while at work, while on the premises of the company or its customers, or while on company business. "Prohibited substances" include illegal drugs, alcohol, or prescription drugs not taken in accordance with a prescription given to the employee.

The Company will conduct drug and/or alcohol testing under any of the following circumstances:

- RANDOM TESTING: Employees may be selected at random for drug and/or alcohol testing at any interval determined by the Company.
- FOR-CAUSE TESTING: The Company may ask an employee to submit to a drug and/or alcohol test at any time it feels that the employee may be under the influence of drugs or alcohol, including, but not limited to, the following circumstances: evidence of drugs or alcohol on or about the employee's person or in the employee's vicinity, unusual conduct on the employee's part that suggests impairment or influence of drugs or alcohol, negative performance patterns, or excessive and unexplained absenteeism or tardiness.
- POSTACCIDENT TESTING: Any employee involved in an on-the-job accident or injury under circumstances that suggest possible use or influence of drugs or alcohol in the accident or injury event may be asked to submit to a drug and/or alcohol test. "Involved in an on-the-job accident or injury" means not only the one who was or could have been injured, but also any employee who potentially contributed to the accident or injury event in any way.

If an employee is tested for drugs or alcohol outside of the employment context and the results indicate a violation of this policy, or if an employee refuses a request to submit to testing under this policy, the employee may be subject to appropriate disciplinary action, up to and possibly including discharge from employment. In such a case, the employee will be given an opportunity to explain the circumstances prior to any final employment action becoming effective.

The following is an example of what a drug/alcohol testing consent form might look like. The Texas Workforce Commission's "Drug and/or Alcohol Testing Consent Form" is designed as a template for a variety of circumstances.[3]

DRUG AND/OR ALCOHOL TESTING CONSENT FORM

EMPLOYEE AGREEMENT AND CONSENT TO DRUG AND/OR ALCOHOL TESTING

I hereby agree, upon a request made under the drug/alcohol testing policy of __________________ (the Company), to submit to a drug or alcohol test and to furnish a sample of my urine, breath, and/or blood for analysis. I understand and agree that if I at any time refuse to submit to a drug or alcohol test under company policy, or if I otherwise fail to cooperate with the testing procedures, I will be subject to immediate termination. I further authorize and give full permission to have the Company and/or its company physician to send the specimen or specimens so collected to a laboratory for a screening test for the presence of any prohibited substances under the policy, and for the laboratory or other testing facility to release any and all documentation relating to such test to the Company and/or to any governmental entity involved in a legal proceeding or investigation connected with the test. Finally, I authorize the Company to disclose any documentation relating to such test to any governmental entity involved in a legal proceeding or investigation connected with the test.

I understand that only duly-authorized Company officers, employees, and agents will have access to information furnished or obtained in connection with the test; that they will maintain and protect the confidentiality of such information to the greatest extent possible; and that they will share such information only to the extent necessary to make employment decisions and to respond to inquiries or notices from government entities.

I will hold harmless the Company, its company physician, and any testing laboratory the Company might use, meaning that I will not sue or hold responsible such parties for any alleged harm to me that might result from such testing, including loss of employment or any other kind of adverse job action that might arise as a result of the drug or alcohol test, even if a Company or laboratory representative makes an error in the administration or analysis of the test or the reporting of the results. I will further hold harmless the Company, its company physician, and any testing laboratory the Company might use for any alleged harm to me that might result from the release or use of information or documentation relating to the drug or alcohol test, as long as the release or use of the information is within the scope of this policy and the procedures as explained in the paragraph above.

This policy and authorization have been explained to me in a language I understand, and I have been told that if I have any questions about the test or the policy, they will be answered.

I UNDERSTAND THAT THE COMPANY WILL REQUIRE A DRUG SCREEN AND/OR ALCOHOL TEST UNDER THIS POLICY WHENEVER I AM INVOLVED IN AN ON-THE-JOB ACCIDENT OR INJURY UNDER CIRCUMSTANCES THAT SUGGEST POSSIBLE INVOLVEMENT OR INFLUENCE OF DRUGS OR ALCOHOL IN THE ACCIDENT OR INJURY EVENT, AND I AGREE TO SUBMIT TO ANY SUCH TEST.

[Important note for the Company. Omit this from any consent form! Remember, "involved in an on-the-job accident or injury" means not only the one who was injured, but also anyone who arguably or potentially contributed to the accident or injury event in any way, that is, the person suspected of causing someone else to get hurt gets tested as well. Testing only accident or injury victims can, in the eyes of some, appear to be a way of discouraging workers from filing workers' compensation claims, and that in turn can have an unfavorable effect on workers' compensation retaliatory discharge lawsuits. See the sample drug/alcohol testing policy for an idea on how to reflect that caution in the policy.]

______________________________ ________________
Signature of Employee Date

____
Employee's Name (Printed)

______________________________ ________________
Company Representative Date

NOTES

1. Reprinted with permission from the Texas Workforce Commission.
2. Texas Workforce Commission, "Drug-Free Workplace Policy." www.twc.state.tx.us/news/efte/drug_free_workplace_policy.html.
3. Texas Workforce Commission, "Drug and/or Alcohol Testing Consent Form." www.twc.state.tx.us/news/efte/drug_and_or_alcohol_testing_consent_form.html.

Appendix G

Pros and Cons of Drug Testing in Schools

"Should Schools Invest in Drug Screening?"[1] is a debate between a teacher who says, "Just say no to drug tests," and a journalist who was a member of a random drug testing committee and argues, "It's working in southern Illinois."

Should Schools Invest in Drug Screening?[2]

NO

Gary D. Askins: "Just say no to drug tests"

President George W. Bush, in his State of the Union message, proposed a $23 million budgetary increase for the testing of public school students. This was not an extension of his No Child Left Behind initiative, this is testing with a Dixie cup. Frankly, I question the efficacy of drug testing and any positive consequences attributed to this "gotcha!" approach to [be] a very serious social question. There are drug users who make laws and legal

YES

John D. Homan: "It's working in southern Illinois"

Some people would say that there is never a good time to adopt a random drug testing policy for students enrolled in extracurricular events. They say it is an infringement on a student's right to privacy. Well, in Herrin, Illinois, we beg to differ. Pardon us for taking such a tough stance with the students. There simply have been too many incidents, too much history involving drug use by students, to sit idly by and do little to solve the problem.

decisions. There are drug users who attend schools. There are drug users who teach in schools. There are drugs users who preach in church. There are drug users who play professional and amateur sports. There are drug users who lambaste other drug users on radio and television. Some of these people are subjected to random drug testing, but most are not. Yes, we as a nation have a drug problem. But will the testing of public school students reduce drug use?

The most recent research, a federally financed study of 76,000 students nationwide, by far the largest to date, found that drug use is just as common in schools with testing as in those without it. "It suggests that there really isn't an impact from drug testing as practiced," Dr. Lloyd D. Johnston, a study researcher from the University of Michigan, said. "It's the kind of intervention that doesn't win the hearts and minds of children."

I don't think students use drugs because they aren't being tested. And a $23 million federal subsidy would enable school districts to test less than 1 percent of our students. If we get selective and target certain student populations by age, ethnic group, sex, participation in certain activities, hairstyles, fashion statements, or musical tastes (or lack thereof), Virtually all schools have drug-related problems of some kind. But when some of the star players are caught smoking weed in their cars just an hour before the big game—or worse yet, getting high in the locker room prior to a game; or even worse, selling illegal drugs to other kids—there is a need for drastic measures. In recent years, we in Herrin have had to deal with these real-life situations, incidents that have divided our community on many occasions and caused irreparable damage. (No town likes to be the butt of jokes from residents in other communities who refer to your fast break offence in basketball as a "jailbreak.") We Herrinites don't want to go through this heartache anymore. Enough is enough. It's time to take our school back.

The Herrin Unit 4 school board took a proactive approach last summer and asked the high school principal and athletic director to form a committee in our community of 10,000 to study the pros and cons of random drug testing. Also lending time to the project were a member of the school board, the district nurse, a police officer, two students, and a handful of business professionals and parents. After carefully studying the law and drug testing policies already in place at other schools in Illinois, we chose what we considered to we will destroy any hope of creating inclusive schools where cooperative teamwork is modeled for problem solving.

If the federal government has some spare money lying around, I would humbly suggest it be spent on programs that have been proven to be effective deterrents to drug abuse: parental involvement, decision-making skill development, extracurricular activities, drug counseling, and peer support groups. If the president, his legislative water carriers, and his drug czar really believe they've found the silver bullet for our drug problem, I think we should start testing them.

Gary D. Askins was a math teacher at Salado High School in Salado, Texas, at the time of the original publication of this article.

be the best guidelines to follow when implementing a random drug testing policy. We wanted to be firm but fair. The idea of establishing the policy in the first place was not to punish students, but rather to deter them from using drugs. It will take months, if not years, to determine the success of the new Herrin drug testing policy, but results in neighboring communities such as Harrisburg, Eldorado, and Mount Carmel are encouraging. If random drug testing is thought to be a heavy-handed solution to the problem in Herrin, so be it. We can live with that. We would rather people know that we run a clean program, at the risk of angering the students, than do nothing and watch the problems escalate.

John D. Homan was a reporter for the Southern Illinoisan *newspaper in Marion, Illinois, at the time of the original publication of this article. He was also a member of the Herrin random drug testing committee.*

NOTES

1. Gary D. Askins and John D. Homan, "Should Schools Invest in Drug Screening?" *American Teacher* 88(7) (April 2004): 4.
2. Published with permission of *American Teacher*.

Appendix H

URL Addresses for the Electronic Privacy Information Center and Fellow Petitioners to the Federal Trade Commission "In the Matter of Facebook, Inc."

In 2010, the Electronic Privacy Information Center (EPIC) filed a thirty-eight-page "Complaint, Request for Investigation, Injunction, and Other Relief" with the Federal Trade Commission against Facebook. EPIC represents fourteen other influential nongovernmental organizations and not-for-profit research bodies, or "Petitioners." The URLs of all the petitioners are listed here.

The Bill of Rights Defense Committee
www.bordc.org

Center for Digital Democracy
www.democraticmedia.org

Center for Financial Privacy and Human Rights
http://financialprivacy.org

Center for Media and Democracy
www.prwatch.org/cmd/index.html

Consumer Foundation of America
www.consumerfed.org

Consumer Task Force for Automotive Issues
www.autoissues.org

Consumer Watchdog
www.consumerwatchdog.org

Electronic Privacy Information Center
http://epic.org

Foolproof Initiative
www.aboutfoolproof.com/general/advocacy.htm

Patient Privacy Rights
http://patientprivacyrights.org

Privacy Activism
www.privacyactivism.org

Privacy Journal
www.privacyjournal.net

Privacy Rights Clearinghouse
www.privacyrights.org

United States Bill of Rights Foundation
www.usbor.org/search/node?keys=privacy&x=8&y=8

U.S. Public Interest Research Groups
www.uspirg.org/about-us

Further Reading

Bailey, Dennis. *The Open Society Paradox: Why the 21st Century Calls for More Openness, Not Less*. Washington, DC: Brassey's, 2004.

Barnett, Emma. "Facebook's Mark Zuckerberg Says Privacy Is No Longer a 'Social Norm.'" *Telegraph.co.uk*, January 2010. Accessed from www.telegraph.co.uk/technology/facebook/6966628/Facebooks-Mark-Zuckerberg-says-privacy-is-no-longer-a-social-norm.html.

Bennett, Colin J. *The Privacy Advocates: Resisting the Spread of Surveillance*. Cambridge, MA: MIT Press, 2008.

Bennett, Colin J., and Rebecca Grant, eds. *Visions of Privacy: Policy Choices for the Digital Age*. Toronto: University of Toronto Press, 1999.

Bennett, Colin J., and Charles D. Raab. *The Governance of Privacy: Policy Instruments in Global Perspective*. Cambridge, MA: MIT Press, 2006.

Bier, Will C., ed. *Privacy: A Vanishing Value?* New York: Fordham University Press, 1980.

Branscomb, Anne Wells. *Who Owns Information?: From Privacy to Public Access*. New York: Basic Books, 1994.

Carroll, Jamuna. *Privacy*. Opposing Viewpoints Series. New York: Greenhaven Press, 2006.

Carroll, John M. *Confidential Information Sources: Public and Private*, 2nd ed. London: Butterworth-Heinemann, 1991.

Cavoukian, Ann, and Tyler J. Hamilton. *The Privacy Payoff: How Successful Businesses Build Trust*. Toronto: McGraw-Hill Ryerson, 2002.

Dimensions of Privacy: A National Research Survey of Attitudes toward Privacy. Garland Reference Library of Social Science, Vol. 98. New York: Garland, 1981.

Dowding, Martin R. "The Internet as a Source of Health Information." *A Patient's Guide to Medical Information* (2003–2004): 14–15.

Eaton, Joseph W. *Card-Carrying Americans: Privacy, Security, and the National ID Card Debate*. Totowa, NJ: Rowman & Littlefield, 1986.

Everett, Margaret. "The 'I' in the Gene: Divided Property, Fragmented Personhood, and the Making of a Genetic Privacy Law." *American Ethnologist* 34(2): 375–86.

Excellence in Access and Privacy: 20 Years in the Making. Information and Privacy Commissioner of Ontario 2007 Annual Report, 1987–2007. Toronto: Information and Privacy Commissioner of Ontario, 2008.

Fay, John. *Drug Testing*. Stoneham, MA: Butterworth-Heinemann, 1991.

Gilliom, John. *Surveillance, Privacy, and the Law: Employee Drug Testing and the Politics of Social Control*. Ann Arbor: University of Michigan Press, 1994.

Harris, Shane. *The Watchers: The Rise of America's Surveillance State*. New York: Penguin, 2010.

Hoffman, Abbie. *Steal This Urine Test: Fighting Drug Hysteria in America*. New York: Penguin Books, 1987.

Holtzman, David H. *Privacy Lost: How Technology Is Endangering Your Privacy*. San Francisco: Jossey-Bass, 2006.

Hutton, Patrick H. "Late-Life Historical Reflections of Philippe Ariès on the Family in Contemporary Culture." *Journal of Family History* 26(3): 395–410.

Jagodzinski, Cecile M. *Privacy and Print: Reading and Writing in Seventeenth-Century England*. Charlottesville: University of Virginia Press, 1999.

Keenan, Kevin M. *Invasion of Privacy: A Reference Handbook*. Santa Barbara, CA: ABC-CLIO, 2005.

Kirkpatrick, Marshall. "Why Facebook Is Wrong: Privacy Is Still Important." *ReadWriteWeb*, January 11, 2010. Accessed from www.readwriteweb.com/archives/why_facebook_is_wrong_about_privacy.php.

Li, Joyce H-S. *The Center for Democracy and Technology and Internet Privacy in the United States: Lessons of the Last Five Years*. Lanham, MD: Scarecrow Press, 2003.

Lyon, David. *Surveillance Studies: An Overview*. Cambridge, UK: Polity Press. 2007.

Martínez, Alemán M., and Katherine Lynk Wartman. *Online Social Networking on Campus: Understanding What Matters in Student Culture*. New York: Routledge, 2009.

McLean, Deckle. *Privacy and Its Invasion*. Westport, CT: Praeger, 1995.

Moore, Barrington, Jr. *Privacy: Studies in Social and Cultural History*. New York: M. E. Sharpe, 1984.

Niblett, G. B. F. *OECD Informatics Studies 2: Digital Information and the Privacy Problem*. Paris: Organisation for Economic Co-operation and Development, 1971.

Ottawa Minister of Supply and Services. *Connection, Community, Content: The Challenge of the Information Highway*. Ottawa, Ontario, Canada: Minister of Supply and Services, 1995.

———. *Preparing Canada for a Digital World*. Ottawa, Ontario, Canada: Industry Canada, 1997.

Palfrey, John, and Urs Gasser. *Born Digital: Understanding the First Generation of Digital Natives*. New York: Basic Books, 2008.

Palm, Elin. "Securing Privacy at Work: The Importance of Contextualized Consent." *Ethics and Information Technology* 11(2009): 233–41.
Plaisance, Patrick Lee. *Media Ethics: Key Principles for Responsible Practice.* Thousand Oaks, CA: Sage, 2009.
Privacy International. "Overview of Privacy." December 16, 2007. Accessed from www.privacyinternational.org/article.shtml?cmd%5B347%D=x-347-559474.
Rule, James B. *Privacy in Peril.* Oxford, UK: Oxford University Press, 2007.
Schoeman, Ferdinand David, ed. *Philosophical Dimensions of Privacy: An Anthology.* Cambridge, UK: Cambridge University Press, 1984.
Skloot, Rebecca. *The Immortal Life of Henrietta Lacks.* New York: Crown Publishers, 2010.
Smith, Janet E. *The Right to Privacy.* Philadelphia, PA: National Catholic Bioethics Center, 2008.
Sofsky, Wolfgang. *Privacy: A Manifesto,* trans. Steven Randall. Princeton, NJ: Princeton University Press, 2007.
Solove, Daniel J. *The Future of Reputation: Gossip, Rumor, and Privacy on the Internet.* New Haven, CT: Yale University Press, 2007.
Strandburg, Katherine, and Daniela Stan Raicu, eds. *Privacy and Technologies of Identity: A Cross-Disciplinary Conversation.* New York: Springer, 2006.
Sykes, Charles J. *The End of Privacy.* New York: St. Martin's Press, 1999.
Thomas, Terry. *Privacy and Social Services.* Brookfield, VT: Ashgate Publishing, 1995.
U.S. Federal Trade Commission. "Gramm-Leach-Bliley Act." Accessed from www.ftc.gov/privacy/privacyinitiatives/glbact.html.
———. "Privacy and Security." Accessed from www.ftc.gov/privacy/.
Weinstein, Karen, and Jason Hanson. *A Practical Guide to Controlling Workplace Substance Abuse in Ontario.* Aurora, Ontario, Canada: Aurora Professional Press, 1995.
Whitaker, Reg. *The End of Privacy: How Total Surveillance Is Becoming a Reality.* New York: New Press, 1999.
Yee, George, ed. *Privacy Protection for E-Services.* Hershey, PA: Idea Group Publishing, 2006.
Young, John B., ed. *Privacy.* New York: Wiley & Sons, 1978.

Index

About the Author

Martin R. Dowding teaches communication policy in the Department of Communication Studies at Wilfrid Laurier University, in Waterloo, Ontario, Canada. He has also taught at the University of British Columbia. Dowding received his PhD in information studies at the University of Toronto in 2002.

www.ingramcontent.com/pod-product-compliance
Ingram Content Group UK Ltd.
Pitfield, Milton Keynes, MK11 3LW, UK
UKHW021034150926
475561UK00003B/97

9 780810 881020